PRACTICAL PROJECTS
for
SELF-SUFFICIENCY

DIY Projects to Get Your Self-Reliant Lifestyle Started

Chris Peterson and Philip Schmidt

COOL
SPRINGS
PRESS
Home and Garden Experts™

MINNEAPOLIS, MINNESOTA

First published in 2014 by Cool Springs Press, an imprint of Quarto Publishing Group USA Inc., 400 First Avenue North, Suite 400, Minneapolis, MN 55401

Cool Springs Press titles are also available at discounts in bulk quantity for industrial or sales-promotional use. For details write to Special Sales Manager at Quarto Publishing Group USA Inc., 400 First Avenue North, Suite 400, Minneapolis, MN 55401 USA. To find out more about our books, visit us online at www.coolspringspress.com.

ISBN: 978-1-59186-595-7

Library of Congress Cataloging-in-Publication Data

Peterson, Chris, 1961-
  Practical projects for self-sufficiency : DIY projects to get your self-reliant lifestyle started : eat, grow, preserve, improve / Chris Peterson.
    pages cm
  ISBN 978-1-59186-595-7 (softcover)
 1. Sustainable living. 2. Home economics, Rural. 3. Small gardens. 4. Farms, Small. I. Title.

 GE196.P48 2014
 640–dc23

                        2013049104

Acquisitions Editor: Mark Johanson
Design Manager: Brad Springer
Layout: Brenda Canales
Front Cover Design: Rob Johnson
Author: Chris Peterson
Contributing Author: Philip Schmidt
Builder/Technical Editor: Eric Smith
Photographer: Tracy Walsh
Illustrator: Bill Kersey, Greg Maxson
Photo Assistance: Susan Storck, Christopher Fultz

Printed in China
10 9 8 7 6 5 4 3 2 1

Contents

Introduction:
Building a
Self-Sufficient Life

Living a more independent lifestyle is a rewarding goal. By learning to do more things yourself you gain control of the how and when and what of modern life. The projects in this book are designed to help you reach the goal of self-sufficient living. The best part is that you don't need to sell your townhome and move to 80 acres in the mountains to make use of these projects. Pick off a few here and there and you can participate in the self-sufficient way of being without making the sacrifices required when living off the grid.

Why aspire to self-sufficiency? Because the pace of modern life can be overwhelming. All too often, the amazing technology that was supposed to free us and make life better and better instead becomes a drain on our money, time, and joy. As we've tried to improve our lives through progress and efficiency, we have ironically gotten further and further from many of the things that make life healthy, rewarding, and fulfilling. It's just a matter of cause and effect. Medical advances that allow for gene therapy are used to create GMO foods of unproven safety. An ever-ready energy supply has ensured that our lives are more comfortable and convenient than ever before; but our environment pays for that convenience in the fallout from fracking, the pollution of

coal-fired power plants, and the occasional devastating oil spill. All the while, modern life seems to demand that we move faster, do more, make more, and consume more. Along the way, we've become less able to do for ourselves, and more in the habit of buying everything we need regardless of the environmental and personal consequences.

And make no mistake, there are consequences. As we continue to fill landfills at an alarming rate, see our water tables and well water increasingly become contaminated, and learn more about how corporate farming is creating a less diverse food-supply chain, the global and environmental benefits of what's come to be known as "self-sufficient living" become more relevant and more apparent. By saving water, raising food that doesn't involve long-distance transport (and all the fuel and pollution that transportation entails), and finding new ways to create what we need using only the energy in our bodies, we're not only helping ourselves, we're helping the world.

Those upsides are attracting growing numbers of people to the self-sufficient lifestyle. The fact that you're reading this book means that chances are, you're one of those people.

Slowly but surely, we're learning that quantity, speed, and convenience are not always equal to quality, wholesomeness, and satisfaction. People across the country are realizing that highly processed food, produced and packaged on an industrial level, is often not as truly good tasting or as good for you as simpler food grown in your own backyard. People are reconnecting with animal husbandry, from raising two or three chickens to a small herd of goats. They are finding the pleasure in working with living things that create resources, such as food and fertilizer, and rediscovering the simple joy of hand-woven textiles made on a loom they built themselves. They are realizing that there is a way to live that is gentler on the eco-systems of which we are so much a part. On a more pragmatic level, they are saving money with what they grow and produce and what they no longer need to buy.

But more than that, they are choosing to live better, more rewarding lives. They are rediscovering the simple pleasure of creating something of worth with their own two hands, of reconnecting with the garden and finding a sense of craftsmanship and purpose in everyday life. These people are creating new traditions for their families and getting reacquainted with timeworn, valuable experiences and skills. This is all part of choosing a richer life.

The homestead may look very different today than in the pioneer days. But what we may lack in acreage we can compensate for in creativity. Growing edibles in containers on a balcony is just one way to pursue your self-sufficient goals in an urban setting.

Home arts like weaving may seem obsolete, but participation in them is growing. If you really want to let your self-sufficiency flag fly, don't just learn to weave: build your own frame loom (see pages 53 to 58).

Hard or soft, apple or pear, homemade cider is pure goodness. But you just can't make it efficiently without a cider press. See pages 13 to 18 for an easy, DIY press you can make.

Thankfully, this movement is not an all-or-nothing proposition. Self-sufficiency doesn't necessarily mean that you need to move completely off the grid and live without modern conveniences or technology. People still need to go to work, attend family events, commute, and spend some down time doing nothing (or whatever they enjoy doing). Other people don't have the skills or inclination to build, much less use, something like a loom. All that's okay. Maybe you don't want to raise chickens, but installing a solar energy source or adding a double-bin composter are more your speed. You can pick and choose; there's no evil in using the computer or watching a ball game on your big screen TV. Self-sufficiency isn't about living in a cave. It's about taking steps to do for yourself, to move back toward simpler, more fulfilling practices in daily life, and to help the environment one step at a time. It's about living healthy and creating a healthier world. In short, it's about changing your life and the world around you in common-sense, achievable and positive ways.

On that note, you should be realistic when you choose which projects in this book you'd like to tackle. If you're up for doing all them, good for you. But it's just as good if you only feel comfortable tackling a few of them right now—or even just one. You can always do more later, and any step you take toward self-sufficiency is a step in the right direction. Even the most modest action is better than overreaching, getting burned out, and giving up on the notion of self-sufficiency altogether.

Raising city chickens is a booming business for today's urban homesteaders, as well as the hobby farmers working in a more rural setting. But keep in mind that for most chicken farmers, it's all about the eggs. We show you how to build your own coop (page 141) and brooder box (page 147).

To give you as much choice as possible, we've included a wide range of projects in the four basic categories of self-sufficient living: storing and preparing food; amenities around the house; gardening; and raising food animals. Within these categories, we've included projects from the amazingly simple to the much more involved. Let's just be clear though: none of these projects will require anything more than moderate DIY and woodworking skills. We've tried to make the simple life as simple as possible to create. No matter how much self-sufficiency you decide to implement in your own life, you'll be changing your life and the world. Do a little or a lot, and you can still feel satisfied that you're doing something. It may seem like a drop in the bucket, but that's exactly how buckets are filled.

Splitting firewood is great exercise and a good way to work off stress, but where will you store it? See pages 47 to 52 for a compact firewood shelter that's also attractive.

Keeping bees is about more than fresh honey and beeswax. The threat of colony collapse is what is really driving the huge surge of interest in backyard apiaries. See pages 151 to 157 for information on building a Langstroth-style beehive for your home.

Food Preparation and Preservation

We depend on our food, just as we do our air and water, to be healthy and wholesome. But increasingly, we have no idea where our food comes from and what is done to it before it reaches us. The farther we move from the source of our food, the more it needs to be processed to get to us. Although shelf life is increased, much can be lost.

That's why there's something wholly satisfying about raising and storing your own food. It's not just that it's amazingly healthy—that much should be obvious. More than that, it's that you're taking steps to ensure that there are no toxins in your family's food. You're also taking empty calories out of your diet—like when you replace soda with fresh-pressed cider. But beyond health, there's the benefit of more flavorful edibles.

Grow heirloom tomatoes and you've given yourself the gift of rich, beautiful, incredibly tasty vegetables that can't be rivaled by what's on offer at the local grocery. Can and preserve part of that harvest, and you'll be enjoying homemade marinara and stews through the winter, while other people are buying factory-canned soups full of preservatives and who knows what else.

But there's another side to self-sufficient food growing, harvesting, and preparation. Once you get outside and start pressing cider, drying fruit, or making your own cheese, you'll discover the vastly enjoyable pleasure of crafting your own wholesome food. The act of walking down a grocery store aisle simply can't compete with slicing up your own fresh-picked cabbage to make a family-favorite cole slaw, or hanging herbs just cut from your garden to make dried additions to your next soup. Get in the habit of tending your plants and working with the harvest they produce, and it quickly becomes the farthest thing from work.

Cider Press

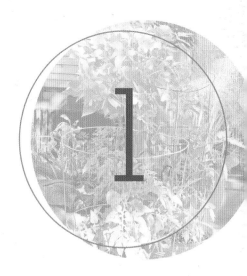

This press is the perfect way to make use of the abundant bounty from apple trees on your property. But even if you don't happen to have your own mini orchard, you can make good use of the wide selection of inexpensive apples available at the local co-op or farmer's market (or any place they sell organic apples).

There are few drinks so satisfying as a well-made, home-brewed apple cider and the process is a simple one. You simply grind the apples into a pulp that you then press to extract the sweet, flavorful juice. If you're only making a small batch, you can chop the apples and process them into pulp in a blender. For larger or multiple loads—if, for instance, you have several trees on your property—you'll want to invest in a full-scale grinder that will make short work of even a large number of apples.

The best ciders incorporate a blend of apples to create an interesting and refreshing flavor profile. Usually, proficient cider makers will include a good amount of very modestly flavored apples (such as Macintosh) as a foundation for the cider, adding tart apples (such as Granny Smiths) to brighten and liven the flavor, and a more flavorful apple to add richness (such as the Orin or Golden Russet). The best way to blend is to crush and press batches of each different apple separately and then blend the ciders so that you can better control the flavor.

When you press and crush the pulp, the cider slowly oozes out of the pulp into the tray below the pressing bucket (a pail in this case). The bucket has to withstand a lot of pressure, and traditionally, press buckets were made from scrap hardwood, with hard staves and hoops and spaces left between the staves for the juice. Because a pressing bucket can be a formidable project in its own right, we've opted for the more convenient 5-gallon plastic pail. These pails are widely available at home centers and hardware stores.

The mash—or crushed apples—is contained within a coarse nylon bag or cheesecloth, which prevents large pieces of apple in the mash from finding their way into the cider. A word of caution about collecting the pressed cider—apple juice can be very acidic, and the acid can react to certain metals, so it's best to catch the juice in a plastic pail and then store it in glass.

A press such as this can process many gallons of delicious cider over a season. It can also be used to crush grapes and extract the juice for homemade wine.

Building a Cider Press

TOOLS AND MATERIALS

Cordless drill

Impact driver (optional)

¼" spade bit

½" spade bit

½" metal drill bit

#8 or 9 countersink bit

Miter saw

Jigsaw

Framing square

Clamps

Hydraulic bottle jack (2 ton)

Nylon mesh bag or yard of cheesecloth

Deck screws 1¼," 2½," 3"

(2) 7 x ½" hex bolts, washers, nuts

(8) 5" self-tapping lag screws with washer heads

(8) 8 x ¼" self-tapping lag screws with washer heads

12 x 16" (or larger) baking pan with 1 to 1½" high sides

(2) 5-gallon food-safe buckets

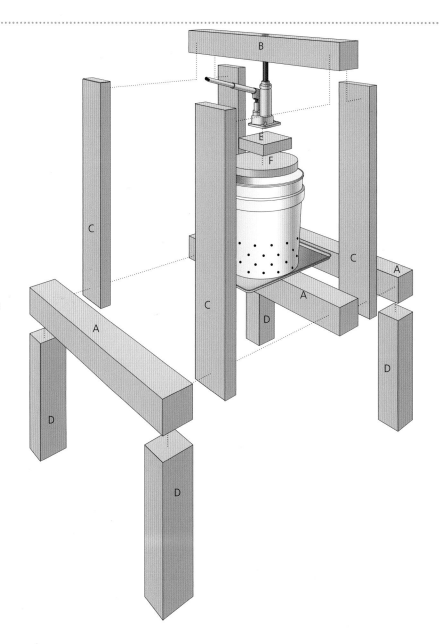

CUTTING LIST

Key	No.	Part	Dimension	Material
A	3	Base boards	3½ x 3½ x 33½"	4 x 4
B	1	Cross brace	3½ x 3½ x 33½"	4 x 4
C	4	Frame supports	1½ x 5½ x 30"	2 x 6
D	4	Legs	3½ x 3½ x 15"	4 x 4
E	2	Press plate	Bucket dia. x ¾"	1 x 12
F	1	Press plate backer	1½ x 5½ x 5½"	2 x 6

*Do not use treated lumber for parts that will contact food products.

Lay out the top cross brace, the center base board and two frame supports. Make sure the frame is square, then attach frame supports with two 3" screws at each corner. Leave room in the center for bolts. Attach the other two frame supports the same way. Drill holes for the carriage bolts that connect the cross brace and frame supports, then bolt the frame together.

Align the outside base boards with the center cross brace. Predrill two ¼" holes at each end of the outside base boards, then fasten the 4 × 4s with two 8" self-tapping lag screws. (If you have an impact driver you can drive the screws in without predrilling.)

(continued)

Position the press frame on the 4 × 4 legs. With the legs properly aligned, drill two pilot holes at each corner of the outside base 4 × 4s, down into the tops of the legs. Screw the base to the legs using 5" self-tapping lag screws.

Trace the bottom of the bucket on the press plates, then trace an inner line with a compass about ⅛" inside of the line. Cut the line with a jigsaw. Offset the grain direction of the two press plates for more strength, then fasten the two plates together with glue and predrilled, countersunk 1¼" screws. Attach a 5 ½" long 2 × 6 to the center of the plates to distribute the force of the jack.

Sand all the edges of the press plate and check the fit. Also cut several short pieces of 4 × 4 to extend the reach of the jack as it pushes down into the bucket.

Mark three ½" drain holes along the front end of the metal tray, spaced 1 inch apart. Use a nail set to mark the center so the drill bit stays put. Clamp the tray to a piece of scrap wood and drill from the inside out. File away any sharp edges and clean thoroughly.

Drill rows of ¼" holes all the way around the 5-gallon bucket, starting 1" above the bottom and continuing to about halfway up. Scrape and sand the holes smooth and wash the bucket.

Chop, grind, and mash the fruit as fine as you can. Pour it into a mesh bag or cheesecloth in the bucket. The finer the apples are ground up, the more cider you'll produce.

Place the pan on the base with the holes over the collection bucket. Place the jack in the center of the press plate. Place a metal plate or large, thick washer on top of the jack to keep the head from pushing into the wood. Slowly compress the fruit with the jack, adding additional 4 × 4 blocks when the jack is too low in the bucket.

TIP

Making the Cider

Once your press is constructed, you're ready to make your first batch of cider. Grind the apples up into mash and place the mash in a nylon mesh press bag (or line the bucket with cheesecloth). Put the bag in the pressing pail and position it so that the press plate is aligned perfectly with the mouth of the pail. You may want to slightly shim the back edges of the back legs, so that the press is tilted forward. This will help the pressed juice run toward the drain holes. Set your collection pail under the drain holes, and pump the jack until juice begins flowing. Continue slowly pumping until no more juice comes out. Now enjoy your first glass of fresh-pressed cider!

Herb-Drying Rack

Herbs are some of the easiest and most enjoyable plants to grow. They can be grown in a small garden plot, in a container garden, or even on a windowsill. The fact is, you can easily grow more than you need with very little effort. Of course, the self-sufficient gardener never lets something go to waste in the garden—and that means making the most of any extra herbs by drying them.

The drying rack described in the pages that follow will give you a place to dry a large harvest of several different herbs. In fact, it's really two drying racks in one. Herbs are dried in two ways: laying down or hanging up. Hardier herbs should be tied in bundles and hung to dry. These include lavender, rosemary, sage, thyme, and parsley and any herb with tough, woody stems. More delicate leaf herbs like basil, mint, and tarragon should be dried flat on a screen. To cover all the bases, the rack in this project includes three lines on top for hanging and three tray slots to hold drying screens. This should provide all of the space you'll need for even a large herb harvest.

We've also included instructions for making your own drying screens. These are basically old-fashioned wood window screens. They are fairly easy to make, and by crafting your own, you control the dimensions. However, you may prefer the ease of buying premade screens, which are available at home centers and hardware stores. If that's the case, simply alter the length of the braces and top to suit the screens you buy (as well as the height of the dadoes). Also, if you're purchasing screens, it's wise to invest in more durable aluminum, rather than fiberglass mesh. Choose aluminum frames for a wide selection of sizes or pick from a much smaller selection of wood-framed screens.

Combining hanging and screen drying, this rack can quickly and efficiently dry any herb you can grow. And it looks just as good as it works.

Building a Herb-Drying Rack

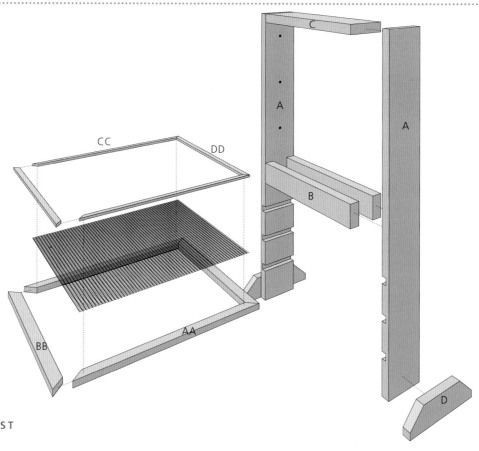

CUTTING LIST

RACK

Key	No.	Part	Dimension	Material
A	2	Sides	1½ x 5½ x 49"	2 x 6
B	2	Braces	1½ x 3½ x 26"	2 x 4
C	1	Top end side	1½ x 5½ x 26"	2 x 6
D	2	Feet end	1½ x 3½ x 12½"	2 x 4 pine

DRYING SCREEN

Key	No.	Part	Dimension	Material
AA	6	Frame end piece	¾ x 1½ x 26⅞"	1 x 2
BB	6	Frame side piece	¾ x 1½ x 20"	1 x 2
CC	6	Molding end	¼ x ¾ x 25⅜"	Wood Screen Molding
DD	6	Molding side	¼ x ¾ x 18½"	Wood Screen Molding

TOOLS AND MATERIALS

Window screen mesh (aluminum or fiberglass)
16-gauge stainless-steel picture hanging wire
(6) 1³⁄₁₆" steel screw eyes
Miter saw

2½" screws
Router with ¾" straight bit
  (or table saw with dado blade)
#5 x ⅝" corrugated fasteners

Cordless drill and bits
Staple gun and staples
¾" brads
Clamps

Mark the side boards for the dadoes. Set up the router with a ¾" straight bit and clamp a cutting guide to the workpiece. Start the first dado cut 6" up from the bottom, ½" deep. Move the cutting guide and make a second pass so the total width is ⅞", or about ⅛" wider than the wood used for the drying rack. (If you use aluminum screen frames, just add ⅛" to the thickness of the frames.) Cut the remaining dadoes. Repeat for the other side board. You can also make the cuts on a table saw using a dado blade.

Measure and mark the placement of the screw eyes on the inside faces of the side boards (same sides as the dadoes). The first pair should be positioned in the center of each side board, 4" from the top. Each of the other two will be positioned 8" below the screw eye above it. Predrill holes and then screw in the screw eyes until they are snug.

Cut and attach the feet with a single screw. Drill pilot holes for the braces, working on one side at a time. Screw the brace to one side panel, and then drill the pilot holes and screw the brace to the opposite side panel. Flip the frame and repeat for the second brace.

(continued)

Tie the picture wire to the screw eyes using pliers to twist the ends and secure the wire. Make sure the wire is tight enough to support the herbs without sagging.

TIP

Herb-Drying

Drying herbs is a simple process, but one that needs to be done correctly to ensure usable herbs. Start by picking the herbs you want to dry before the first buds on the herb begin to bloom. Once the plant flowers, the herb will usually become bitter. Pick only healthy whole leaves and stems; avoid wilted, yellowed or diseased parts of the plant.

- When drying herbs, keep the dryer out of direct sun, because direct sun can diminish the flavor of the herbs.
- Speaking of flavor, keep in mind when it comes time to use the herbs that dried herbs usually have much more intense flavor than the same herb fresh—often by a factor of four.
- Crumble your dried herbs and store them in airtight containers, in a cool, dry and dark location.

Stand the dryer up on a level surface. Check for plumb and mark the proper position of each foot. Drill pilot holes and secure each foot firmly along the marked lines, with 2 to 3 additional screws.

Project Detail: How to Make the Drying Screen

Cut 45° miters in the ends of the frame and molding pieces. Check the fit and adjust as necessary.

Assemble the frame, fastening the pieces together with corrugated staples (inset) driven at each corner.

Fasten the screen with ⁵⁄₁₆" staples every few inches. Pull the screen tight as you staple. Cut away the excess screen when you're done stapling.

Position the molding on the inside edge of the frame. Nail it to the frame with brads. Repeat the process to construct the two remaining screens. Coat the frames with linseed oil or other non-toxic sealant.

Solar Oven

There are many effective ways to make a solar cooker—one website devoted to the subject features dozens of photos of different types sent in by people from all around the world. The basic principle is so fundamental that it is easily adapted to a range of styles. We settled on this particular design mostly because it's low-cost to build, working with wood is often easier than manipulating metal, and the unit can cook about any meal you might need to make. However, it's easy enough to modify this design to suit your own food preparation needs.

The cooker is big enough to hold two medium-size pots. All the pieces are cut from one 8-foot 2 × 12 and a sheet of ¾-inch plywood. (The cooker would work just as well with ¼-inch plywood, but we used ¾-inch because it made it simpler to screw the corners and edges together.) The base is made from 1½-inch thick lumber for ease of construction and for the insulation value of the thicker wood, but thinner material would also work.

The foil we used was a type recommended for durability and resistance to UV degradation by an independent research institute. Unfortunately, it was expensive, and if you're just starting out you may want to do a trial run with heavy-duty aluminum foil. Although foil looks a little dull, it actually reflects solar rays almost as well as specially polished mirrors.

In operation, the cooker is the height of simplicity. The sun's rays reflect off the foil sides and are concentrated at the base of the cooker, where they are absorbed by the black pot. The glass cover (or clear oven cooking bag) helps hold heat and moisture in the pot. The cooker should face the sun. Raise or lower the box depending on the time of year so that you catch the sunlight straight on. Shim the wire rack as needed to keep the pot level.

A solar cooker is an incredibly useful appliance that exploits the limitless energy in sunshine to cook meals large and small.

Types of Solar Cookers

There are many different types of solar cookers. Really, the only requirement is that the sun's rays be captured and focused on whatever is being cooked. Beyond that, the actual construction of the unit can be left to the imagination. However, the most common and popular types of solar cookers can be divided between three groups.

Parabolic Concentrators

Sometimes called curved concentrators, these are a more sophisticated design, but they accommodate only one cooking pot at a time in most cases. However, the shape effectively focuses the sun's rays much better than other types of solar cookers, resulting in higher cooking temperatures. These cook faster, but must be monitored more closely to ensure proper cooking. Crude versions can sometimes be adapted from retired satellite dishes or other parabolic devices.

Box Cookers

These are probably the most popular type of solar cooker because they are so easy to build. The shell can be even be made from found wood or other scavenged materials of odd sizes (which probably accounts for the prevalence of this type of cooker in the third world and impoverished areas). Basically, all you need is a box with a reflective surface inside, and a reflective lid. The box is positioned facing south, and opened at an angle that best directs the sunlight down into the cavity of the box. This type of cooker can be built small or large, is highly portable, and can be constructed to accommodate specifically the dimensions of the cookware that the user already owns.

Panel Cookers

These can be considered a hybrid of the other two styles of cookers. These are a fundamental design that is easy to construct and works well—sometimes better than a box cooker. They are available as kits from self-sufficiency and survivalist manufacturers, but with a little bit of thought and effort, one can easily be constructed from scratch. Be prepared to experiment with the angling of the panels to find exactly the orientation that will work best for your location and situation.

Building a Solar Oven

Key	No.	Part	Dimension	Material
A	2	Base side	1½ x 11¼ x 19"	2 x 2 pine
B	2	Base end	1½ x 11¼ x 16"	2 x 2 pine
C	1	Bottom	¾ x 19 x 19"	¾" ext. grade
D	1	Adjustable leg	¾ x 10 x 17"	¾" ext. grade
E	1	Hood back	¾ x 20 x 33¾"	¾" ext. grade
F	1	Hood front	¾ x 10 x 25¼"	¾" ext. grade
G	2	Hood side	¾ x 20 x 31¼"	¾" ext. grade
H	1	Lens	¼ x 17¼ x 17¼"	Tempered glass

TOOLS AND MATERIALS

Straightedge

Circular saw

Jigsaw or plunge router

Tape measure

Drill/driver with bits

Speed square

Stapler

Eye and ear protection

#8 countersink bit

¾" × 4 × 8-ft. BC or better plywood

2 × 12 × 8-ft. SPF SolaReflex foil or heavy-duty aluminum foil

Bar clamps

1⅝ and 2½" deck screws

Clear silicone caulk

Mid-size black metal pot with glass top

Wire rack

No-bore glass lid pulls

¼ × 2" hanger bolts with large fender washers and wingnuts

SOLAR OVEN

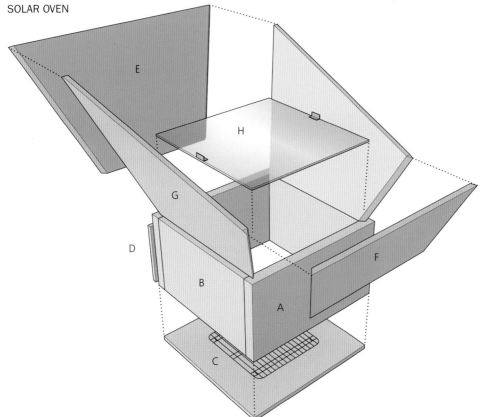

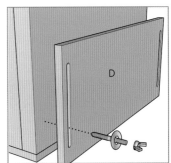

Cut the four 2 × 12 base pieces to length according to the cutting list. Arrange the base parts on a flat work surface and clamp them together in the correct orientation. Check for square and adjust as needed. Drill pilot holes and fasten the pieces together with 2½" deck screws.

Lay a sheet of plywood on the work surface with the better side facing up. Mark and cut the bottom first. Rest the full sheet of plywood on a couple of old 2 × 4s.

To create the panels that form the reflector you'll need to make beveled cuts on the bottom and sides so the panels fit together squarely. Mark two 20 × 76" long pieces, measuring from the two factory edges so the waste will be in the middle. Set your circular saw base to 22½°, then cut along the line you drew at 20". Cut the other piece starting from the opposite end of the plywood. You should end up with two mirror-image pieces.

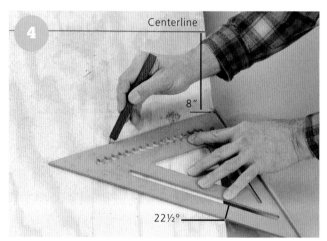

Reset your saw base to 0°, then cut each 20"-wide panel in half so you have four 20 × 38" panels, each with one beveled 38" edge. With the beveled edge facing up and closest to you, draw a centerline at 18" on each panel, then make marks on the beveled edges at 8" on both sides of the centerline. Position a speed square so it pivots at the 8" mark, then rotate the speed square away from the centerline until the 22½° mark on the speed square meets the top of the beveled edge. Draw a line and use a straightedge to extend the line to the other edge (the factory edge) of the plywood. Repeat at the other 8" mark, flipping the speed square and rotating it away from the centerline so the lines create a flat-topped triangle. Set the base of your circular saw at 40°, then cut along the angled lines. Mark and cut the remaining three panels in the same fashion.

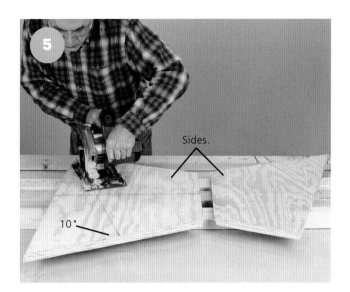

Finish cutting the reflector parts to final size and shape. Tip: After you've laid out your cutting lines, set the work piece onto a pair of old 2 × 4s. Tack the work pieces to the 2 × 4s with finish nails, driven into the waste area of the panels. Keep the nails at least a couple of inches from any cutting line. Set your saw so the cutting depth is about ¼" more than the thickness of the work piece and then make your cuts.

Assemble the reflector. Brace two of the reflector sides against a square piece of scrap plywood clamped to the work surface, then join the edges with screws driven into countersunk pilot holes. Repeat for the other two pieces. Join the two halves together with four screws at each corner, completing the reflector. The bottom edges should be aligned. The top edges won't match perfectly, so sand them smooth.

Compound Miter Corner Cuts

The sides of this solar cooker box are cut with the same basic technique used to cut crown molding. Instead of angling the crown against the miter saw fence in the same position it will be against the ceiling—a simple 45° cut that is easy to visualize—you have to make the compound cuts with the wood lying flat, which makes it mind-bendingly difficult to visualize the cut angles. For the dimensions of this cooker, a 40° bevel cut along the 22½° line will form a square corner. If you change the 22½° angle, the saw cut will also change.

If you remember your geometry, you can work all this out on paper. But bevel guides on circular saws are not very precise, and 40° on one saw might be more like 39° on a different brand; test cuts are the best way to get the angle right. Make the first cuts a little long and then try them out.

The easiest way to avoid a miscut is to lay all the pieces out with the bases lined up and the good side of the plywood up. Mark the 22½° lines for the sides, then cut the 40° angles on one edge of all four pieces. Next, flip the piece around and cut the 40° angle on the other side. Remember, the 40° cut should angle outwards from the good side of the plywood, and the pieces should all be mirror images.

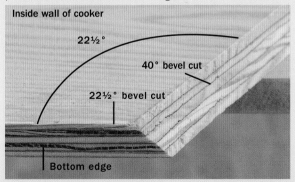

Inside wall of cooker
22½°
40° bevel cut
22½° bevel cut
Bottom edge

(continued)

Cut the adjustable leg with parallel slots so the leg can move up and down over a pair of hanger bolts, angling the cooker as necessary. Outline the slots so they are ⅜" wide (or slightly wider than your hanger bolt shafts). Locate a slot 2" from each edge of the adjustable leg. The slots should stop and start 2" from the top and bottom edges. Cut the slots with a jigsaw or a plunge router.

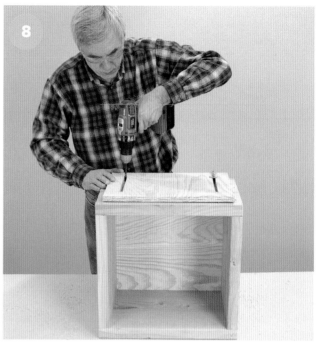

Screw the plywood bottom to the base. Set the adjustable leg against one side of the base, then drill guide holes and install the hanger bolts to align with the slots. Center the bolts at the same height: roughly 2½" up from the bottom of the box. Use large fender washers and wing nuts to lock the adjustable leg in position.

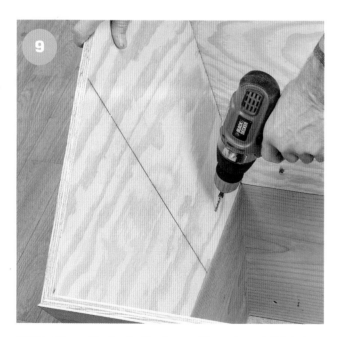

Fasten the reflector to the base with countersunk 2½" deck screws. Angle the drill bit slightly as you drill to avoid breaking the plywood edge. Use two screws per side.

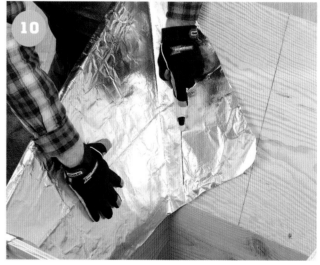

Cut pieces of reflective sheeting to fit the sides of the reflector as well as the base. You can use heavy-duty aluminum foil, but for a sturdier option try solar foil. Cut the pieces large enough to overlap at the edges.

Glue the reflective sheeting inside the base and reflector, overlapping the sheets. Use contact cement or silicone caulk and staple the edges to reinforce the glue (use diluted white glue with a paintbrush instead of contact cement if you're using aluminum foil.) Smooth out the reflective material as much as possible; the smoother the surface is, the better it will reflect light.

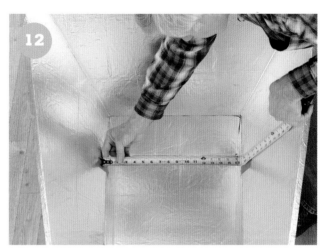

Take measurements to double-check the glass lid size. Ideally, the lid will rest about 1" above the top opening of the box. Order glass with polished edges. You can also use a clear plastic oven bag instead of the glass. Either will trap heat and speed up the cooking.

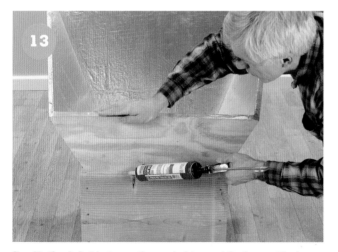

Caulk the joint between the angled top and the base with clear silicone caulk. Set a wire rack inside the oven to keep the cooking pot slightly elevated and allow airflow beneath it.

Getting a Handle on Glass

Because it is virtually impossible to lift the glass lid from above, you'll need to install handles or pulls designed to attach to glass (available from woodworking hardware suppliers). The simplest of these require no drilling. You squeeze a bead of clear, 100 percent silicone into the U-channel of the lid handle, then slide the handle over the edge of the glass.

Solar Fruit Dryer

This all-metal drying rack has more of an industrial look than most homespun wood versions, but there are good reasons for opting for metal. First, when you're working with food, you want a material that is washable and heat-resistant. Metal meets both of these requirements, while wood really meets neither, at least not over the long haul. Also, when you're dealing with extended exposure to sunlight, you want a material that's UV-resistant and won't warp, dry out, or deteriorate. Metal wins again.

Buying new materials for this metal dryer may cost more than using old scrap wood and some window screening, but the slightly higher price is the only drawback. Building the dryer is easy and straightforward (saving you time), and the dryer will outlast any appliance in your house (saving money in the long run).

You can customize the size of the dryer to fit your needs and drying locations. The "shelves" are stainless steel cooling racks, the kind used by home bakers for cooling cakes and cookies. Buy as many racks as you like in the desired size, then build the dryer framework to fit the racks. Choose grid-style racks with thin wires and the smallest openings available (½-inch or smaller). The metal reflector at the bottom of the dryer reflects heat up toward the racks to speed the drying process.

When determining the size of your dryer, consider the amount of food you're likely to dry at one time, as well as the interior capacity of your oven. Solar dryers are designed to use the sun for power, of course, but it never hurts to have the option of slipping the dryer into the oven—for a little extra drying or just as a handy place to store the dryer at night.

Drying is a perfect way to preserve a large fruit harvest. It's also a very easy process when you have a fruit dryer that taps the power of the sun, like the one in this project.

TIP

Tips for Solar Drying

Although it seems like a very simple process, solar drying fruit is not just a case of drying out something that is juicy. If not done correctly, you can wind up with a big harvest of inedible leathery pieces.

- Start with fresh, fully ripened—but not overripe—fruit or vegetables.
- Cut foods evenly for consistent drying; some foods such as figs, grapes, and plums should be pierced, not sliced, while others can be sliced or chopped for drying.
- Pre-treating fruits in a solution of ascorbic acid, citric acid, or lemon juice can minimize discoloration and help prevent unwanted bacterial growth.
- Rotate racks as needed so foods dry at roughly the same time.
- If insects are a problem, cover the dryer loosely with a piece of flexible window screen, cheesecloth, or even mosquito netting; just be aware that this will block some sunlight and airflow, adding to the drying time.
- Allow dried foods to condition for 4 to 10 days before storing.
- Store dried food in airtight glass or plastic containers kept in a cool, dark place.
- Contact a local extension office for tips and recommendations on drying foods specific to your region.

Building a Solar Dryer

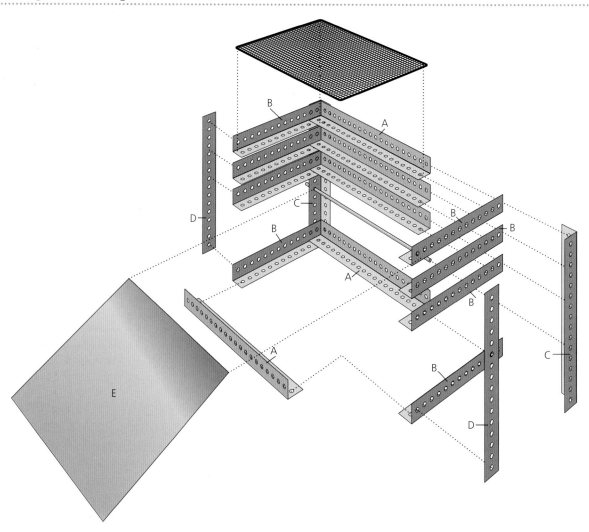

CUTTING LIST

Key	No.	Part	Dimension	Material
A	5	Shelf (front/back)	16½"	1½ x 1½" slotted steel angle
B	8	Shelf (side	10½"	1½ x 1½" slotted steel angle
C	2	Rear upright	13⅛"	1½ x 1½" slotted steel angle
D	2	Front upright	13⅛"	1½ slotted steel flat bar
E	1	Reflector	16½ x 12"	Sheet Metal

TOOLS AND MATERIALS

Marking pen
Reciprocating saw or jigsaw with metal-cutting blade, or hacksaw
Metal file
Wrenches
Tin snips
Stainless steel cooling racks
(5) 4-ft. x 1½ x 1½" or 1¼ x 1¼" slotted steel angle*

(1) 3-ft. x 1½" or 1¼" slotted steel flat bar*
(20) ¾ x ⁵⁄₁₆" hex bolts with washers and nuts (sized for holes in steel angle and flat bar)
Hardwood dowel (sized for holes in steel angle)
Scrap wood and screws (as needed)
*Use plain-steel angle and bar, not galvanized or zinc-plated.

Design the dryer frame to fit your cooling racks. Add ½" to ¾" to the width and depth of each shelf space to make sure the racks have enough room to slide easily along the shelf angles. Also allow space for the heads of the bolts that hold the frame together. Lay out the cuts for the two rear uprights on the steel angle; mark the cuts for the two front uprights on the flat steel bar. The lengths of these pieces are all the same and should equal the overall height of the dryer minus the thickness of the angle material (the front and lower rear crossbars will sit below the uprights). *Note:* The trick to laying out the cuts is to align the holes in the corresponding pieces so that all of the holes are lined up in the finished assembly. You can mark and cut each piece as you go, using the cut piece as a template for aligning the holes and marking the cut for the next piece.

File the ends of each piece to remove any burrs and sharp edges. Mark and cut two shelf angles and the upper rear crossbar, again making sure the holes are aligned between like pieces.

Cut the four uprights. You can cut the pieces with a hacksaw, reciprocating saw, or jigsaw with a metal-cutting blade, although a cut-off saw (a metal-cutting chop saw, not a standard miter saw) is ideal.

(continued)

Drying Your Harvest ... and Then Some

Once you've completed your new solar fruit dryer, the hard part's over. That's because the process of drying fruits and vegetable could not be simpler. Just cut and arrange whatever it is you need to dry, and let the sun do the work. Keep the dryer in direct sun as much as possible for best results. Most fruits will dry completely in one day. Other sturdier foods, such as tomatoes, should be dried for two days.

Don't limit yourself. The list of potential fruits and vegetables for drying is a long one, and may even spur you to plant and grow new vegetables and fruits. A short list of some of the more unusual dried fruits and veggies includes:

Heirloom tomatoes
Plantains
Yellow onions
Mushrooms (wild and otherwise)
Zucchini (and just about any other squash)

You can even use the dryer to dry herbs in a pinch (although you'll find it easier to use the Herb Dryer on page 19). The idea is the same either way: have dried food ready to use out of season. All you need to do to bring the dried vegetables back to life is water and time. Simply soak them for 10 to 30 minutes in warm water or oil.

Of course, you can also eat anything you dried in its dried state. Most dried fruits add an incredible element sprinkled over cereal or on top of a bowl of yogurt. Eat sundried tomatoes plain, with sprinkling of salt and a drizzle of avocado oil.

Temporarily assemble the uprights, base, and one or two crossbars to make sure that everything fits well, the holes are properly aligned, the fruit dryer is square, and the rack fits. The bolt heads protrude less than the nuts, so they should go on the inside (or shelf-side) of the frame; washers and nuts go on outside of the uprights and the underside of the crossbar.

If everything goes together properly, cut the remaining pieces, making sure to line up the holes. The easiest way to do this is to use one piece as a template for length and hole locations. If you have a good saw and sharp metal cutting blade you can cut several pieces at once. Use a file to smooth the metal edges.

Complete the dryer-frame assembly, hand-tightening the bolt connections. Then tighten each bolt connection with wrenches. You may need to flip the cooling racks over if the legs get in the way.

Cut the sheet metal for the reflector panel to size with tin snips, or a jigsaw with a metal cutting blade if the metal is too thick for snips (sandwich the metal between thin pieces of plywood for a smoother cut). Insert a dowel through the rear uprights at the height desired, then rest one end of the panel on top of the dowel to reflect sunlight and radiate heat toward the racks.

Tip

You can change the angle of the reflector panel to catch the most sunlight or to follow the path of the sun during the day. If the metal is thin and too flexible, fasten it to a piece of plywood, securing the metal with small screws driven through the panel's top side or with silicone adhesive. You can also use plywood or even cardboard wrapped with foil.

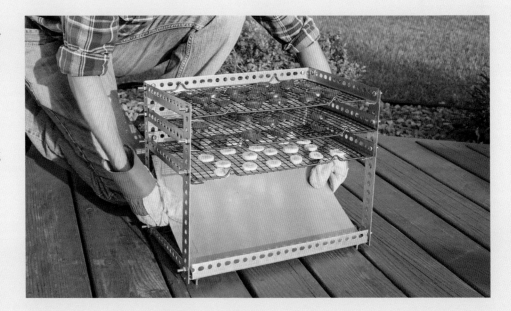

Homestead Amenities

The most important word in homestead is "home." After all, everything you're doing in a move toward self-sufficiency is aimed at making your home a better place to live. You can actually consider homesteading the improvement of your many homes—the world, your region, and the plot of land that holds that structure where you lay your head at night. This section is, in the final analysis, all about that last one.

As anyone knows, a home can either be warmly inviting, comforting and wonderful, or cold and off-putting, and never quite settled. The amenities in this chapter focus on moving your home toward the former rather than the latter. You see, when you make your home—including the inside and outside—more functional, you make it a nicer place to live.

You can consider these practical amenities. Having a handy place to stack and season your firewood, a homemade clothesline, or a metal shed for storage, is all about convenience. Projects like these also often provide viable alternatives to using expensive appliances that are energy hogs. Do a load of laundry in a manual laundry machine and you save electricity even while you discover the meditative bliss of losing yourself in 40 minutes of non-taxing labor performing an essential household task. Beyond convenience and the other rewards of these projects lies something else. Something that isn't quite as tangible, but to anybody who values self-sufficiency and a return to a simple life, is just as important. That is handmade craftsmanship.

Surrounding ourselves with conveniences isn't hard. A few hours spent at an appliance store can do that. But surrounding ourselves with conveniences that give us a connection to our home and remind us that yes, we can do for ourselves . . . well those are simply the best type of conveniences and true homestead amenities.

Backyard Firepit

5

A firepit is a backyard focal point and gathering spot. The one featured here is constructed around a metal liner, which will keep the firepit walls from overheating and cracking if cooled suddenly by rain or a bucket of water.

The liner here is a section of 36-inch-diameter corrugated culvert pipe. Check local codes for stipulations on pit area size. Many codes require a 20-foot-diameter pit area.

Ashlar wall stones add character to the firepit walls, but you can use any type of stone, including cast concrete retaining wall blocks. You'll want to prep the base for the seating area as you dig the firepit to be sure both rest on the same level plane.

TOOLS AND MATERIALS

Wheelbarrow
Landscape paint
String and stakes
Spades
Metal pipe
Landscape edging
Level
Garden rake

Plate vibrator
Metal firepit liner
Compactable gravel
Top-dressing rock (trap rock)
Wall stones
Eye protection and work gloves

Some pointers to consider when using your firepit include: 1) Make sure there are no bans or restrictions in effect; 2) Evaluate wind conditions and avoid building a fire if winds are heavy and/or blowing toward your home; 3) Keep shovels, sand, water, and a fire extinguisher nearby; 4) Extinguish fire with water and never leave the fire pit unattended.

Building a Backyard Firepit

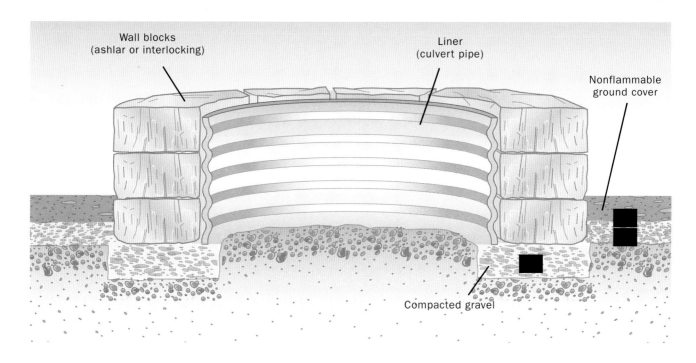

Wall blocks
(ashlar or interlocking)

Liner
(culvert pipe)

Nonflammable
ground cover

Compacted gravel

Plan View: Firepit

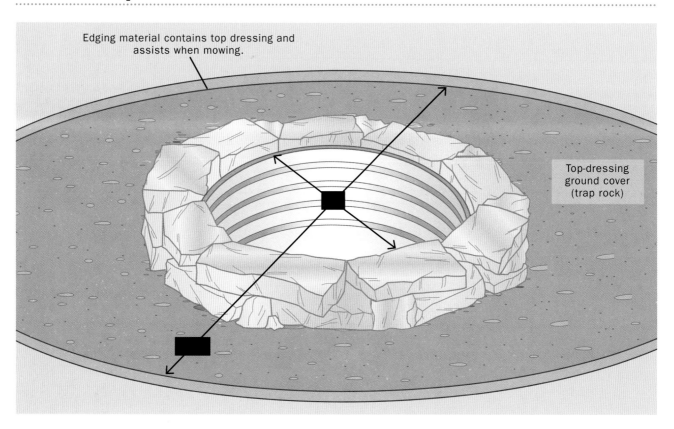

Edging material contains top dressing and
assists when mowing.

Top-dressing
ground cover
(trap rock)

Outline the location for your firepit and the firepit safety area by drawing concentric circles with landscape paint using a string and pole for guidance.

Remove a 4"-deep layer of sod and dirt in the firepit and safety areas (the depth of the excavation depends on what materials you're installing in the safety zone.)

Dig a 4"-deep trench for the perimeter stones that will ring the pit liner.

Fill the trench for the perimeter stones with compactable gravel and tamp thoroughly. Then scatter gravel to within 2½" of the paver edging top throughout the project area. It is not necessary to tamp this layer at this time.

Place your metal fire ring so it is level on the gravel layer and centered around the center pole.

Arrange the first course of wall blocks around the fire ring. Keep gaps even and check with a level, adding or removing gravel as needed.

Install the second course of retaining wall block, taking care to evenly stagger the vertical joints on the first and second courses. Add the remaining courses.

Compact the compactable gravel in the seating/safety area using a rented plate vibrator.

Place and compact a layer of top-dressing rock in the seating/safety area to complete the firepit.

Firewood Shelter

6

Everyone knows that wood burns best when it's dry. But properly dried, or "seasoned," firewood isn't just about making fires easy to start and keep burning. Seasoned wood burns hotter and cleaner than unseasoned ("green") firewood, resulting in more heat for your home, reduced creosote buildup in your chimney, and lower levels of smoke pollution going into the air.

Seasoning freshly split wood takes at least six months in most areas, but the longer you can dry it the better. The best plan is to buy firewood (or cut and split your own) as early as possible and stack it in a well-ventilated shelter with a good roof. This shelter will keep your wood covered through snow and rain while providing ample ventilation and easy access to the stack. It also looks better than any prefab shelter and is easy to modify with different materials or dimensions.

An optional feature is a storage locker at either end of the structure, perfect for storing your axe, gloves, and other tools and supplies. A simple bin or locker at the other end can hold kindling or provide more protected storage space. The roof trusses add some custom detailing and actually simplify the construction. You can top the roof with fiberglass panels, as shown, or any other type of roofing material.

The shelter is sized to hold a half-cord of split firewood cut to 16-inch lengths, and stacked two deep. If you use shorter logs, you can stack them two or three deep. For longer logs or to accommodate a whole cord of wood, you can easily modify the shelter dimensions to fit (see Resizing Your Shelter, right).

Resizing Your Shelter

A cord of split and stacked firewood measures 4 x 4 x 8 ft., or 128 cubic ft. Standard log lengths are 12, 16, and 24", with plenty of variation in between (they're logs, after all, not trimwork). Sizing your shelter depends on the length of your logs, how much wood you want to store, how you want to stack it (two-deep, three-deep, etc.), and how much roof coverage you'd like extending over the sides of the stack.

Modifying this shelter design is simple. First determine the floor platform size and the height between the floor and the roof—these dimensions give you the overall wood storage capacity. The rest of the structure can be sized and built as you go, as all of the other elements are based on the spans between the corner posts. For a significantly longer shelter design, add full-height intermediate posts and additional trusses to strengthen the roof assembly; for a much deeper (more square-shaped) structure, use intermediate posts and/or larger lumber for the trusses and roof beams.

A shelter like this is a handsome addition to a yard or alongside the house, and will keep your firewood nice and dry as it ages. Add storage lockers at either end of the shelter to make it even more useful.

Building a Firewood Shelter

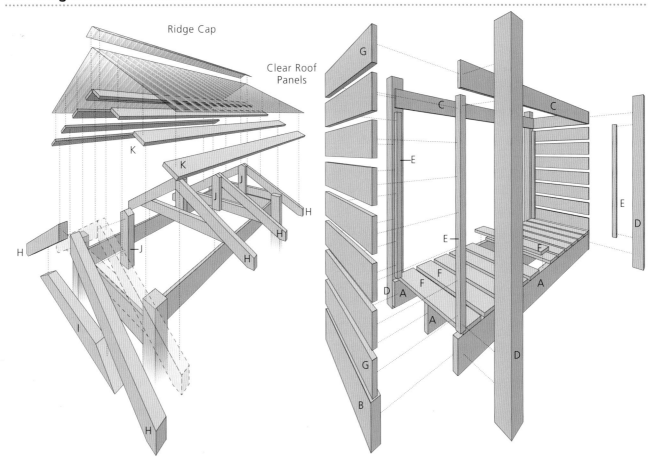

Ridge Cap

Clear Roof Panels

CUTTING LIST

Key	No.	Part	Dimension	Material*
A	3	Floor Beams	1½ x 7¼ x 81½"	2 x 8
B	2	End Beam	1½ x 7¼ x 26"	2 x 8
C	2	Roof Beam	1½ x 5½ x 81½"	2 x 6
D	4	Corner Post	3½ x 3½ x 67"	4 x 4
E	4	Corner Cleat	1½ x 1½ x 48	2 x 2
F	12	Deck Board	¾ x 5½ x 28"	1 x 6
G	16	Siding	¾ x 5½ x 28"	1 x 6
H	8	Top chords	1½ x 3½ x 30"	2 x 4
I	4	Bottom chords	1½ x 3½ x 36"	2 x 4
J	4	Truss Center Post	1½ x 3½ x 14½"	2 x 4
K	8	Purlins	¾ x 3½ x 92"	1 x 4

* All lumber should be pressure-treated; posts and floor beams should be rated for ground contact. All hardware must be corrosion-resistant for outdoor exposure.

TOOLS AND MATERIALS

Hammer

Tape measure

Carpenter's square

4-ft. level

Circular saw with wood- and metal-cutting blades

Reciprocating saw or handsaw

Cordless drill and bits

Clamps

Socket wrench

Miter saw (optional)

8d galvanized siding nails

Deck screws 2, "2½," 3½"

(16) 6 x ⅜" carriage bolts with washers and nuts

⅞" roofing screws with neoprene washers

Joist hangers (for 2 x 8) with recommended fasteners (2)

Joist hanger nails

Rafter ties

16d galvanized common nails

Fiberglass roofing panels

Assemble the frame with 3½" deck screws driven through the side beams and into the ends of the end beams. Install the floor center beam using joist hangers and joist hanger nails or screws. Measure from diagonal to diagonal in both directions to make sure the frame is square, then temporarily screw a board across two corners to hold it in place. Set the floor frame on a flat, level surface, on 1"-thick spacers.

Position the posts so they extend ¾" beyond the ends, to leave room for the 1 × 6 slats. Clamp each corner post to the outside of the frame, check for plumb and square, and then screw it in position with two screws through the 2 × 8 (remember to leave room for bolts). Drill two ⅜" holes through the posts and side beams, angling the drill so the bolts go from the middle of the 4 × 4 to the open part of the 2 × 8. Anchor each post with two carriage bolts.

Mark the center line across the floor beams, then position and screw down the deck boards, starting ¾" to each side of the center line. Space the boards 1⅜" to 1½" apart and fasten with 2½" screws. Overhang the beams about ½" on each side. Check and adjust the spacing as you get close to the ends—pressure-treated wood can vary as much as ⅛" in width, depending on how dry it is.

(continued)

Clamp each roof beam to the opposing corner posts so that the top edge of the beam is 3½" below the top ends of the posts, and the ends of the beams are ¾" in from the outside faces of the posts. Hold the beams in place with a 2½" deck screw at each end, then drill holes and fasten the beams to the posts with ⅜" carriage bolts.

Enclose the openings on the ends of the shelter with 1 × 6 slats secured to 2 × 2 cleats mounted to the inside faces of the posts. Install the cleats ¾" back from the outside faces of the posts so that the slats are flush with the post faces. Space the slats roughly 1¾" apart.

Miter the end cuts on the top chords at 30° on the miter saw. Mark the ends of the bottom chord at 60° with a speed square, then cut with a circular saw. Hold the center post of the truss in place and mark it for cutting. Build the trusses on a flat surface, fastening the top chords to each other and to the bottom chord with 3½" screws. Use 2½" screws to fasten the center post.

Mark the outside faces of the corner posts 3½" down from their top ends. Clamp the two outer trusses to the posts with the bottoms of the trusses on the 3½" marks, then fasten them with 16d galvanized nails.

Position the remaining two trusses on top of the roof beams, spacing them evenly, and screw them to the roof beams using rafter ties.

Nail the purlins across the rafters on both sides with 8d nails. Make sure the rafters are spaced evenly before you nail. The ends of the purlins should extend 3" beyond the outside trusses.

Cut sections of clear roofing sheets to the desired overhang. Clamp the sheets to a solid base and cut with a thin-kerf fine-cutting carbide blade (or a ferrous metal-cutting blade for metal). Sand or file sharp or jagged edges. Fasten the roofing to the purlins using roofing screws with neoprene washers. Overlap the sheets and screw through both pieces along the joint. Install ridge caps using the same screws.

Frame Loom

7

Weaving your own textiles can be incredibly relaxing, enjoyable, and fulfilling. It's a way to reclaim a heritage craft and create beautiful fabric pieces, from scarves to rugs. The trick is to build your skills on a small loom first, and then progress to a larger, more complicated loom. This naturally means starting small, but the idea is to build on your successes, and avoid the frustration that can come from handling a more sophisticated apparatus before you're ready.

Frame looms like the one in this project are ideal for the beginner or intermediate weaver. They are easy to handle, portable, and small enough that they don't take up much room. Just the same, you'll be able to create decorative fabric panels for hanging, small runner rugs, scarves, and even panels that can be sewn together to create more involved projects like a quilt.

The construction of this loom is simple and straightforward. The example here is a fairly standard size, but don't be afraid to resize the dimensions to suit your own needs and preferences. Just be careful not to make it too big or the frame will have a tendency to flex as you work, making the weaving more difficult. We've also included legs on this frame loom to make weaving more comfortable. Adjust the position so that you can sit comfortably and weave without excessive reaching or fumbling.

As the name implies, you begin by building a fundamental frame to which the supporting (or "warp") fibers will be secured. The "weft" threads that run horizontally are then woven through these warp threads. This is the basic process of any loom—the technique just becomes more involved the bigger and more complex the loom. The terms associated with loom weaving can be a little confusing to the beginner, so we've included a glossary to keep things straight. No matter what words you use, however, the result will be a fabric that you've created with your own hands—no fabric store or mill necessary!

Create marvelous handicrafts with a simple frame loom like this one. It's easy to use and will help develop your weaving skills, should you ever want to step up to a standalone loom and bigger textiles like rugs and bedspreads.

Building a Frame Loom

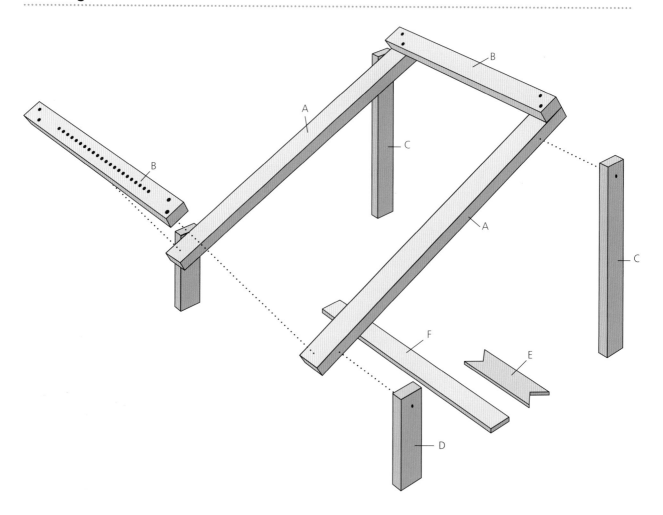

CUTTING LIST

Key	No.	Part	Dimension	Material
A	2	Frame Sides	¾ x 1½ x 24"	1 x 2
B	2	Frame Ends	¾ x 1½ x 18"	1 x 2
C	2	Back legs	¾ x 1½ x 12"	1 x 2
D	2	Front legs	¾ x 1½ x 5"	1 x 2
E	1	Shuttle	¼ x 1½ x 6"	Mull strip*
F	1	Shed stick	¼ x 1½ x 18"	Mull strip

* Can also be made from a paint stir stick.

TOOLS AND MATERIALS

Measuring tape
Cordless drill and bits
Handsaw or utility knife
1½" finish nails

2½" machine screws and matching wing nuts (10–32)
Rubber non-slip furniture leg pads
Construction adhesive

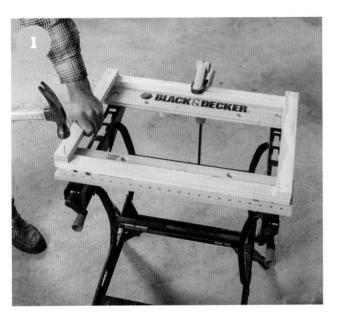

Set the frame sides flat on a clean, level work surface and align the frame ends across either end of the sides. Drill pilot holes and nail the ends to the sides using two finish nails at each corner. Check for square as you work and adjust as necessary.

Mark and drill holes through the tops of the four legs and through each frame side. The legs are attached 2" in from each end of the frame. The holes need to be the same diameter or just slightly bigger than the machine screws you've selected. After the holes are drilled and tested, mark the legs for each side and remove the bolts.

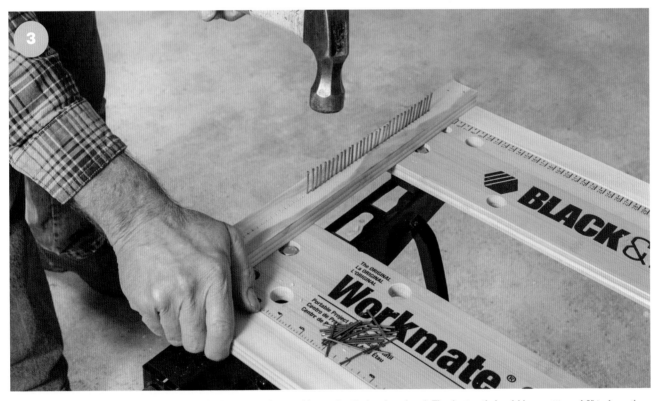

Mark the guide nail locations along the bottom end piece (the end with the short legs). The first nail should be positioned 3" in from the end, with nails every ¼" along the face of the end piece. The last nail will be located 3" in from the opposite end. Mark all the locations, then predrill the holes so the wood doesn't split. Drive a finish nail at each point, halfway into the wood.

(continued)

Drill a ⁵⁄₃₂" hole in the shuttle face, ¾" from the end, and centered between the edges. Repeat on the opposite side. Mark lines from the corners to the hole, and use a jigsaw or handsaw to cut a triangle from the end of the shuttle. Repeat on the opposite side.

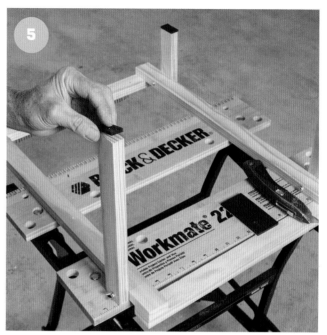

Attach the legs to the loom frame with the machine screws and wing nuts. Cut the rubber pads to the fit the bottom of the legs and glue them in place with construction adhesive. These will keep the frame from sliding when you are weaving.

Weaving Terms

There's a whole language around working with a loom. Once you learn them, the terms are pretty common sense, and they're necessary if you ever graduate to a more complex freestanding loom.

Warp: This is the main set of threads or yarn fibers that run vertically up the loom. The word is also used to describe the process of attaching these threads.

Weft: The yarn or fibers that run horizontally between the warp threads.

Heddle: To make things easier, avid weavers use this tool to maintain a space between alternating warp threads. This makes it much easier to weave the weft in and out of the warp. The project described here uses a shed stick for the same function.

Shuttle: You can weave the weft by hand, or do what most weavers do and wrap the yarn or fiber around this handy tool. It's basically just a flat stick with grooves or cutouts, around which the yarn is wrapped. The shuttle is then passed through the warp to quickly create the weave.

Shed: The space you create with a heddle or spacer stick—through which the shuttle and weft yarn passes—is called a shed.

Using Your Loom

The basic idea behind this loom—and any loom for that matter—is to interweave yarn in perpendicular directions to create strong textile panels. Although yarn is the most commonly used fiber, other fibers can be used for different purposes, such as weaving placements for a dining table. In any case, begin by tying one end of the yarn around the bottom end (the end with the nails) of the frame. Secure it with a double slip knot and wind the warp under the top end, over the top end, then under the bottom end and back over, so that the warp looks like a figure 8. Use the brads as guides to create regular spacing between the strands of yarn. Slid the shed stick between the warp near the top end of the loom, then move it down toward the bottom end and turn it on edge, creating a space for the shuttle to pass through. Tie the end of the weft to the side of the frame at the bottom, then pass the shuttle through the warp

and tamp the weft down to the bottom. For the next weft, slide the shed stick from the other side, over and under the opposite warps. In other words, where the weft went under a warp, it should now go over it. This can be painstaking work if the warp goes through every nail, but can go much quicker if the warp is spaced more widely. After the shed stick is all the way through, turn it on edge again and pass the shuttle back through. Then pull the weft tight, push it to the bottom, and repeat the first step. Work back and forth to create the weave, tamping down each weft row with the shed stick, so that it's snug to the row beneath it. (There are specialized tools called "beaters" for this purpose, but on a small loom like this one, the shed stick works just as well.) When you're done, untie or cut the warp at either end, and either leave the loose strands, trim them, or finish the piece with a fabric edge band.

SHED STICK

SHUTTLE

Solar Still

With local water supplies increasingly under threat from contaminants such as the runoff from large agricultural operations, ensuring a safe water supply is more of a concern than ever—especially for homeowners who draw their water from a local well. This still can be a great backup, and one more way to ensure self-sufficiency.

The box is built from ¾-inch BC-grade plywood, painted black on the inside to absorb heat. We used a double layer of plywood on the sides to resist warping and to help insulate the box, with an insulated door at the back and a sheet of glass on top. As the box heats up, the water evaporates and heavier contaminant in the vapor is left behind.

Finding the right lining to hold the water inside the box as it heats and evaporates can be a challenge. The combination of high heat and contaminants can corrode metals faster than usual and cause plastic containers to break down or off-gas, imparting an unpleasant taste to the distilled water. The best liners are glass or stainless steel, although you can also coat the inside of the box with two or three coats of black silicone caulk (look for a type approved for use with food). Spread the caulk around the bottom and sides with a taping knife. After it dries and cures thoroughly, just pour water in—the silicone is impervious to the heat and water.

We chose to paint the inside black and use two large glass baking pans to hold the water. Glass baking pans are a safe, inexpensive container for dirty or salty water, and they can easily be removed for cleaning. We used two 10 × 15-inch pans, which hold up to 8 quarts of water when full. To increase the capacity, just increase the size of the wooden box and add more pans.

The operation of the distiller is simple. As the temperature inside the box rises, water in the pans heats up and evaporates, rising up to condense on the angled glass, where it slowly runs down to the collector tube and then out to a container.

The runoff tube is made from 1-inch PEX tubing. Stainless steel can also be used. However, use caution with other materials—if in doubt, boil a piece of the material in tap water for 10 minutes, then taste the water after it cools to see if it added any flavor. If it did, don't use it.

A solar still is a very simple device for ensuring clean, drinkable water—courtesy of the sun.

Building a Solar Still

CUTTING LIST

Key	No.	Part	Dimension	Material
A	1	Base liner	¾ × 23¾ × 19"	Rigid insulation
B	1	Base	¾ × 23¾ × 19"	Plywood
C	1	Inner front frame	¾ × 5¾ × 19"	Plywood
D	1	Outer front frame	¾ × 5⅝ × 20½"	Plywood
E	2	Base	1½ × 3½ × 22½"	2 × 4
F	1	Inner rear frame	¾ × 3 × 20½"	Plywood
G	1	Door inner	¾ × 5⅞ × 20½"	Plywood
H	1	Door outer	¾ × 9 × 20½"	Plywood
I	2	Outer side frame	¾ × 9⅛ × 5⅛ × 26¾"	Plywood
J	2	Inner side frame	¾ × 8⅞ × 5⅝ × 24½"	Plywood
K	1	Window	27¼ × 22 × ⅛"	Tempered glass
L	1	Drain tube	1"	PEX tubing, cut to length

TOOLS AND MATERIALS

Drill/driver with bits	Clamps	Knob or drawer pull	(2) 10 × 15" glass baking pans
Circular saw	Tape measure	27¼ × 22 × ⅛"	Wood glue
Speed square	(1) ¾" × 4 × 8-ft. sheet of	(minimum) glass	1¼", 2", 2½" deck screws
Straightedge	BC exterior plywood	Silicone caulk	Painter's tape
Caulk gun	(2) 1½" galvanized hinges	High-temperature black paint	Sliding bolt catch
Utility knife	Self-adhesive weatherseal (8 ft.)	1" PEX tubing	

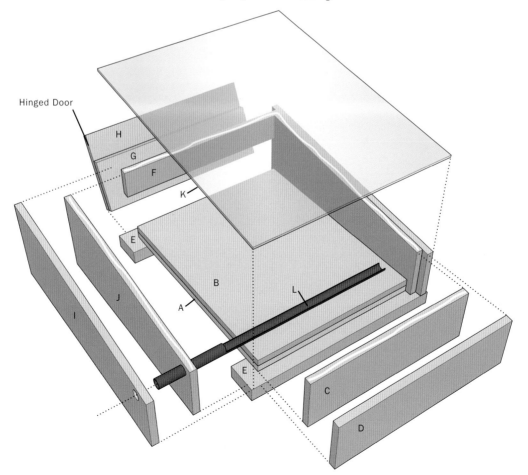

Hinged Door

Mark and cut the plywood pieces according to the cutting list. Cut the angled end pieces with a circular saw or tablesaw set to a 9° angle.

Cut the insulation the same size as the plywood base, then screw both to the 2 × 4 supports with 2½" screws.

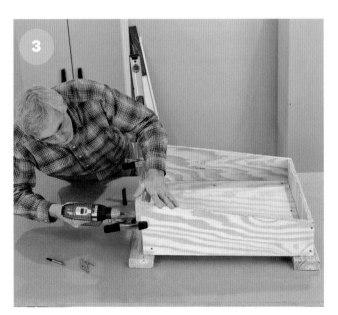

Screw the first layer of front and side pieces to the base and to each other, then add the back piece. Predrill the screws with a countersink bit.

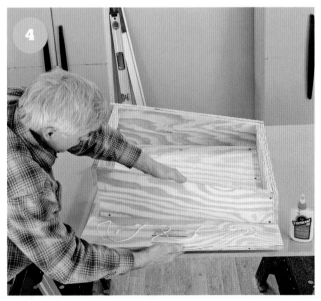

Glue and screw the remaining front and side pieces on, using clamps to hold them together as you predrill and screw. Use 1¼" screws to laminate the pieces together and 2" screws to join the corners.

(continued)

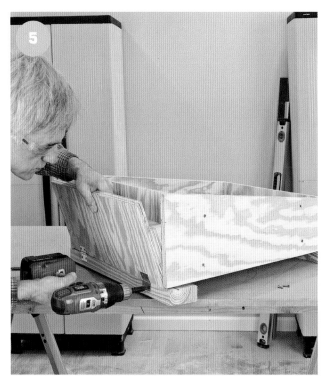

Glue and screw the hinged door pieces together, aligning the bottom and side edges, then set the door in position and screw on the hinges. Add a pull or knob at the center.

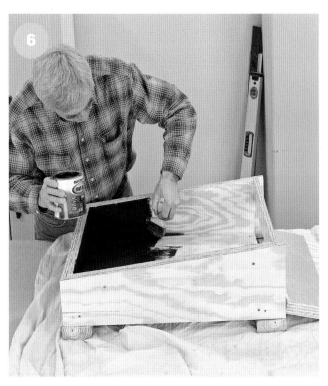

Paint the inside of the box with black high-temperature paint. Cover the back and the door with reflective foil glued with contact cement. Let the paint dry for several days so that all the solvents evaporate.

Apply weatherseal around the edges of the hinged door to make the door airtight.

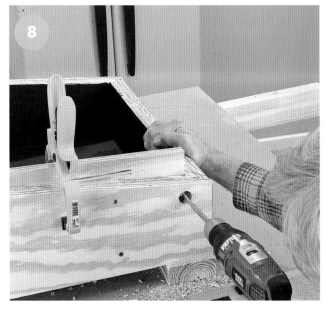

Drill a hole for the PEX drain. The top of the PEX is ½" down from the top edge. Clamp a scrap piece to the inside so the drill bit doesn't splinter the wood when it goes through.

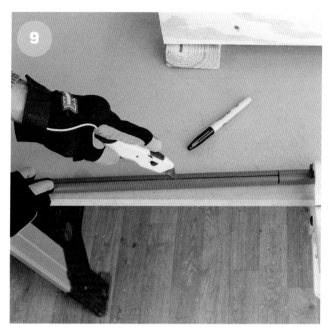

Mark the first 19" of PEX, then cut it in half with a utility knife. Score it lightly at first to establish the cut lines.

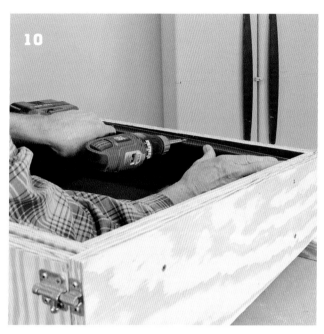

Drill three ⅛" holes in the side of the PEX for screws, then insert the PEX through the hole. Butt it tight against the other side, then screw it in place, sloping it about 1¼".

Wipe a thick bead of silicone caulk along the top edge of the PEX to seal it against the plywood.

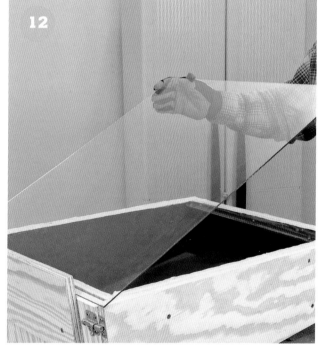

Shim the box level and tack a temporary stop to the top edge to make it easy to place the glass without smearing the caulk. Spread a generous bead of caulk on all the edges, then lay the glass in place. Tape it down around the edges with painter's tape, then let it set up overnight.

Manual Laundry Washer

Today's high-efficiency washers and driers are marvels of modern technology. They use less electricity and water than their predecessors, and include more features than ever. However, for all their improvement on past models, they still use a significant amount of energy to run (especially when someone does a small, "quick" load—you know who you are), as well as good deal of precious water.

What's more, washing clothes hasn't changed. The whole idea remains astoundingly simple: agitate the garments in soapy water for a period of time until dirt loosens and releases from the clothes. That basic function doesn't necessarily need a high-tech solution. If you're looking for something more sustainable, more environmentally friendly, and cheaper, you've found it—a simple, manual laundry machine.

This unit is not a challenge to build. All you need are a few basic carpentry tools, a few pieces of hardware and a couple hours to assemble it. You can build it from components you'll find at any well-stocked hardware store or large home center. The capacity probably won't rival the drum for your current washer, but is certainly large enough to handle most loads of laundry or animal blankets.

Once you've put your washer together, actually doing a load of laundry entails plunging the handle repeatedly for about 20 minutes. The machine makes great use of the lever principle so anyone—even someone with moderate strength and stamina—can easily wash a load of laundry by hand. Use biodegradable soap and you can merely empty the bucket in your landscaping as gray water. Hang the clothes up to dry (use the Clothesline Trellis on page 91) and you're done!

Save electricity, get a little exercise, and conserve water with this handy manual clothes washer. The ingenious lever action ensures that clothes are properly agitated and thoroughly washed.

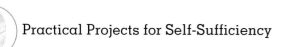

Building a Manual Laundry Machine

TOOLS AND MATERIALS

Cordless drill and bits
Table saw or circular saw
Jigsaw
5-gallon plastic bucket with lid
(4) 2½" x ⅝ corner braces
(1) ¼ x 6" machine screw and nut or wing nut
(1) ¼ x 4" machine screw and nut or wing nut
Deck screws 3," 3½"
¾" stainless-steel wood screws for corner braces
¾" stainless-steel bolts, nuts and washers for pail lid agitator
Large bucket or tub

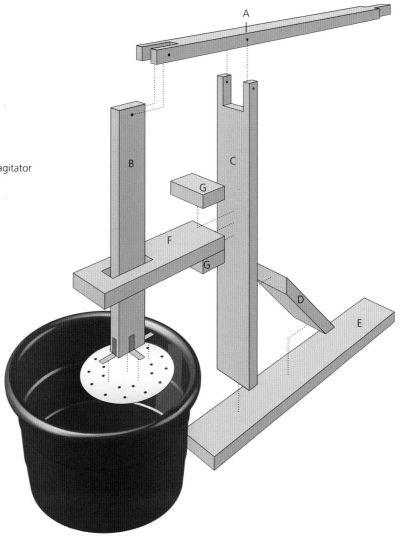

CUTTING LIST

Key	No.	Part	Dimension	Material
A	1	Handle	1½ x 3½ x 51"	2 x 4
B	1	Plunger	1½ x ½ x 25"	2 x 4
C	1	Support	1½ x 5½ x 36"	2 x 6
D	1	Brace	1½ x 5½ x 15"	2 x 6
E	1	Base	1½ x 5½ x 40"	2 x 6
F	1	Guide	1½ x 5½ x 18"	2 x 6
G	2	Cleats	1½ x 3½ x 5½"	2 x 4

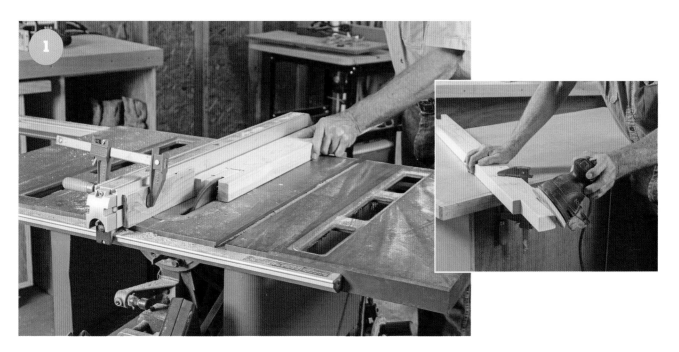

Cut the slot in the end of the handle to accept the plunger by making multiple passes with the table saw. Clamp a stop to the fence so that all the cuts are the same length. The slot should be cut centered on the face of the handle, 1½" wide by 4" deep. Clean the slot out with a chisel after cutting it and sand smooth. Cut and sand the opposite end of the handle to make a grip that's 1½" wide by 5" long. (If you don't have a table saw, just cut the slot with a jigsaw and square the end with a chisel.)

Cut the plunger to length. Mark a hole for the plunger at 1¾" from the side and 1" from the end so that it lines up with the end of the handle and extends ¼" beyond the top of the handle. Drill a ¼" hole centered in the side of the handle slot, 1¾" from the end. Continue the hole through the plunger and opposite slot. Use a drill press if you have one to get a straight hole; otherwise, mark and drill the holes in both sides of the handle, run the bit all the way through to straighten the hole, then drill through from alternate sides of the handle through the plunger. (If the hole is angled too much it may cause the plunger to bind when you move it up and down. If this happens, just redrill the holes with a 5⁄16" bit.)

Mark and cut out the slot in the end of the handle support board. The slot should be centered on the face of the support, 3½" wide by 3" deep. Drill the ¼" pivot hole through the sides of the slot ¾" from the end and ¾" from the side. Drill the matching hole in the handle at 13¾" from the center of the hole plunger hole.

(continued)

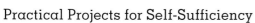

Attach the base to the opposite end of the support with 3½" deck screws. Miter the ends of the brace 45° and fasten it to the base and support with toenailed 2½" deck screws.

Mark the guide hole for the plunger arm in one end of the guide board. The outer edge of the hole should be 2½" from the end of the board. The hole will be a rectangle, 2 × 5½", with the long sides parallel to the long sides of the guide. Center it on the face of the guide board and drill holes at all four corners. Use a jigsaw to cut out the hole.

Screw the guide to the support, on the opposite side from the brace, using 3½" deck screws. It should be positioned 18" up from the base. Screw one cleat above and one cleat below the guide, snug to it, using 3½" deck screws. Also screw the support and braces together for more rigidity.

Attach the handle to the support with a ¼ × 6" machine screw and bolt or wing nut. Use washers on either side. The bolt should slide through the hole in the handle fairly easily. If it doesn't, run the drill bit through a few more times.

Attach 2½ × ⅝" stainless-steel corner braces to the sides and faces at the bottom end of the plunger. Screw the braces in place with 1" stainless steel wood screws. Use a utility knife to cut the pail lid along the inside seam, then remove the lip. Center the end of the plunger on top of the lid and mark the location of the holes in the corner braces. Drill the holes for the corner braces, and then drill a varied pattern of about 20 additional ⅜" holes spaced evenly around the lid. This will allow water to pass through when you are agitating the laundry.

Attach the pail lid to the end of the plunger with ¾" stainless-steel bolts, washers and nuts. Slide the plunger arm up through the guide hole in the guide. Secure the tongue at the end of the plunger in the handle groove using a 4" machine screw, a bolt or wing nut, and washers. Check the operation of the handle and plunger and adjust as necessary. You can use a 5-gallon bucket for washing small loads or a larger tub for dropcloths, horse blankets, and other large items.

Pet Door

Pet doors are available in a variety of styles, colors, materials, and mechanisms. Install one and your dog can go outside whenever he wishes with nary a lift of a finger from you. But don't even consider installing a dog door to the outdoors if you don't have a securely fenced-in yard. To avoid the potential for someone opening the gate in your yard and unintentionally letting your dog loose, locked gates are also a must.

One of your biggest decisions when faced with the plethora of dog door styles will be choosing between the electronic and the manual dog door. If cost is a factor, you're going to lean toward the manual; if security is your greatest concern, then your best bet is the electronic door.

The electronic door is made of hard plastic or Plexiglas, and it responds to an infrared signal from a key attached to the dog's collar. It can emit a hum when activated, which is disconcerting to some dogs at first. When shopping for an electronic dog door, pay attention to the specs; some electronic doors open in only one direction.

Some dogs will go through the door right away without a problem, but most need to have some level of introduction or training. It's important that you introduce your dog to this contraption slowly and cheerfully. If you know a friendly dog who already uses a dog door, invite him over; dogs do learn from each other. Barring a friendly canine teacher, there are some simple techniques that with enough patience are bound to work.

Before you install the flap, take the one item that is most irresistible to your dog and go to the other side of the door. Slowly wave the goody just under your dog's nose and lure him toward you through the door. Give your dog the come command in a cheerful and encouraging manner.

Once your dog is stepping through the dog door like it's no big deal, install the flap. Go to the side of the door opposite your dog, pull the flap toward you just a bit, and lure your dog as you did when the door was wide open. Do this a few times so your dog gets used to the feel of the flap against his body, then just call your dog to go through the door, flap and all. Any time you hit a snag, go back to the last point your dog behaved reliably, and train slowly from there.

A pet door gives your pets freedom and can make life easier for you as well.

Installing a Pet Door

TOOLS AND MATERIALS

Measuring tape
Torpedo level
Drill and bits
Jigsaw
Screwdriver

Pliers
Hacksaw
Pet door
Masking tape
Caulk

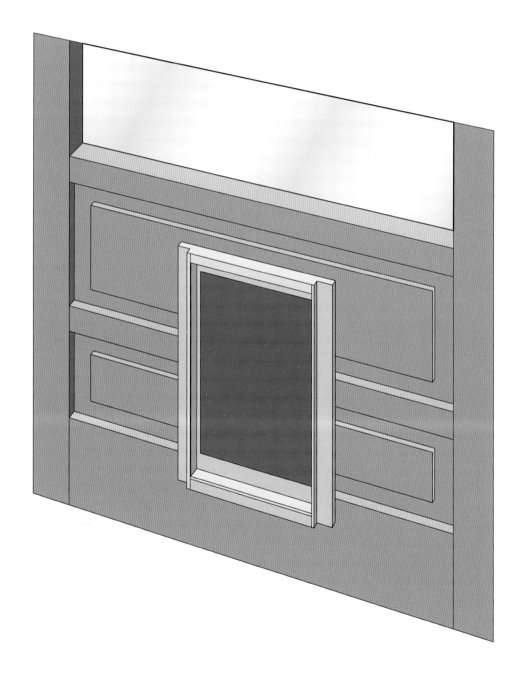

Measure the largest animal that will be using your door and purchase a pet door that is a little larger. Measure a dog's breadth across the shoulders and depth between shoulder and bottom of rib cage. Center the template that comes with the pet door on the lower middle of the human door. The ideal height of a dog door top is about 2" above the standing dog's shoulders. For structural reasons, the cutout should not fall below 3" from the bottom of the human door. Center the template with a measuring tape. Level with a torpedo level, tape in place, and draw cutout lines and bolt hole locations. Remove the template.

Drill the prescribed bolt holes. Next, drill starter holes just inside the corners of the cutout rectangle for the jigsaw blade. If the door is metal, pound a dimple into the surface at each hole location with a nail, and then drill through with progressively larger bits until you can fit your saw blade through. Cut along the side and bottom cutout lines with a jigsaw. Cut the top side last. Tape the cutout in the door as you go to support it, and to keep it from splintering or tearing.

If the pet door straddles a rail and a recessed panel or panels, you'll need to even out the opening so the door has a flat installation surface. Measure the depth of the panel relative to the rails with a ruler and a board held across the rails of the door. Rip-cut strips of blocking to this thickness out of ¾"-thick stock. Measure and cut the blocking to length to fill low panel areas and glue pieces of blocking around the opening. Put blocking on each side of the opening for pet doors with both an interior and an exterior trim kit.

Insert inside and outside door components and bolt it together through the bolt holes. Trim the bolts and attach the flap according to manufacturer's instructions. The exact installation requirements will vary. If needed, tape the pet door flap up until your pet becomes accustomed to using the door.

Metal Kit Shed

11

You don't have to have construction expertise to build a good-looking and useful addition to your yard. If you need an outbuilding but don't have the time, expertise, or inclination to build one from scratch, a kit shed is the answer. Today's kit sheds are available in a wide range of materials, sizes, and styles—from snap-together plastic lockers to Norwegian pine cabins with divided-light windows and loads of architectural details.

Equally diverse is the range of quality and prices for shed kits. One thing to keep in mind when choosing a shed is that much of what you're paying for is the materials and the ease of installation. Better kits are made with quality, long-lasting materials, and many come largely preassembled. A shed from a kit is a known quantity—the look, the storage space, and the complexity of it are apparent beforehand.

The metal shed described here is typical. It measures 8 × 9 and comes complete with every piece you'll need for the main building precut and predrilled. All you need is a ladder and a few hand tools for assembly. The pieces are lightweight and maneuverable, but it helps to have at least two people for fitting everything together.

As with most kits, this shed does not include a foundation as part of the standard package. It can be built on top of a patio surface or out in the yard, with or without an optional floor. To help keep it level and to reduce moisture from ground contact, it's a good idea to build it over a bed of compacted gravel. A 4-inch-deep bed that extends about 6 inches beyond the building footprint makes for a stable foundation and helps keep the interior dry throughout the seasons.

Before you purchase a shed kit, check with your local building department to learn about restrictions that affect your project. It's recommended—and often required—that lightweight metal sheds be anchored to the ground. Shed manufacturers offer different anchoring systems, including cables for tethering the shed into soil, and concrete anchors for tying into a concrete slab.

A shed like this one is an incredibly handy storage feature for just about any homestead. It can be used to store game feed, yard tools and supplies, or even firewood.

Building a Kit Shed

Wooden shed kits generally follow the same, simple-to-build construction style. Using the structural gussets and framing connectors, you avoid tricky rafter cuts and roof assembly. Many hardware kits come with lumber cutting lists so you can build the shed to the desired size without using plans.

Metal doesn't mean ugly when it comes to kit sheds. As this unit clearly shows, these homestead additions add both abundant space and understated style that doesn't detract from the look of the yard.

Shed Features to Consider

Here are some of the key elements to check out before purchasing a kit shed:

Materials

Shed kits are made of wood, metal, vinyl, various plastic compounds, or any combination thereof. Consider aesthetics, of course, but also durability and appropriateness for your climate. For example, check the snow load rating on the roof if you live in a snowy climate, or inquire about the material's UV resistance if your shed will receive heavy sun exposure. The finish on metal sheds is important for durability. Protective finishes include paint, powder-coating, and vinyl. For wood sheds, consider all of the materials, from the framing to the siding, roofing, and trimwork.

Extra Features

Do you want a shed with windows or a skylight? Some kits come with these features, while others offer them as optional add-ons. For a shed workshop, office, or other workspace where you'll be spending a lot of time, consider the livability and practicality of the interior space, and shop accordingly for special features.

What's Included?

Many kits do not include foundations or floors, and floors are commonly available as extras. Other elements you're not likely to find are roof coverings (often the plywood roof sheathing is included but not the building paper, drip edge, or shingles); paint or finish (some sheds come prefinished though). Most shed kits include hardware (nails, screws) for assembling the building, but always check this to make sure. Easy-assembly models may have wall siding and roof shingles already installed onto panels.

Prepare the building site by leveling and grading as needed, and then excavating and adding a 4"-thick layer of compactible gravel. If desired, apply landscape fabric under the gravel to inhibit weed growth. Compact the gravel with a tamper and use a level and a long, straight 2 × 4 to make sure the area is flat and level.

Begin by assembling the floor according to the manufacturer's directions—these will vary quite a bit among models, even within the same manufacturer. Be sure that the floor system parts are arranged so the door is located where you wish it to be. Do not fasten the pieces at this stage. Note: Always wear work gloves when handling shed parts—the metal edges can be very sharp.

Once you've laid out the floor system parts, check to make sure they're square before you begin fastening them. Measuring the diagonals to see if they're the same is a quick and easy way to check for square.

Fasten the floor system parts together with kit connectors once you've established that the floor is square. Anchor the floor to the site if your kit suggests. However, some kits are designed to be anchored after full assembly is completed. Follow the manufacturer's recommendations.

(continued)

Begin installing the wall panels according to the instructions. Most panels are predrilled for fasteners, so the main trick is to make sure the fastener holes align between panels and with the floor.

Tack together mating corner panels on at least two adjacent corners. If your frame stiffeners require assembly, have them ready to go before you form the corners. With a helper, attach the frame stiffener rails to the corner panels.

Install the remaining fasteners at the shed corners once you've established that the corners all are square.

Lay out the parts for assembling the roof beams and the upper side frames and confirm that they fit together properly. Then, join the assemblies with the fasteners provided.

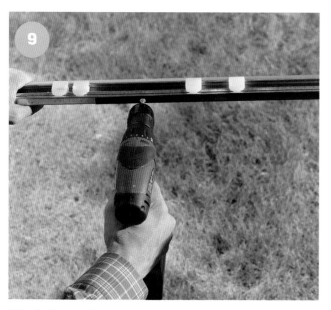

Attach the moving and nonmoving parts for the upper door track to the side frames if your shed has sliding doors.

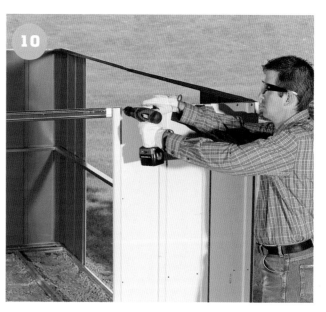

Fasten the shed panels to the top frames, making sure that any fastener holes are aligned and that crimped tabs are snapped together correctly.

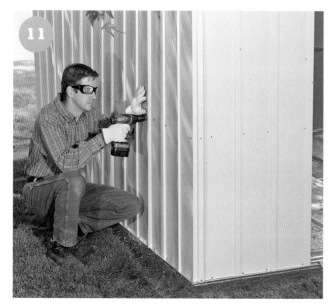

Fill in the wall panels between the completed corners, attaching them to the frames with the provided fasteners. Take care not to overdrive the fasteners.

Fasten the doorframe trim pieces to the frames to finish the door opening. If the fasteners are colored to match the trim, make sure you choose the correct ones.

(continued)

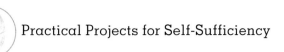

Insert the shed gable panels into the side frames and the door track and slide them together so the fastener holes are aligned. Attach the panels with the provided fasteners.

Fit the main roof beam into the clips or other fittings on the gable panels. Have a helper hold the free end of the beam. Position the beam and secure it to both gable ends before attaching it. Drive fasteners to affix the roof beam to the gable ends and install any supplementary support hardware for the beam, such as gussets or angle braces.

Begin installing the roof panels at one end, fastening them to the roof beam and to the top flanges of the side frames.

Apply weatherstripping tape to the top ends of the roof panels to seal the joints before you attach the overlapping roof panels. If your kit does not include weatherstripping tape, look for adhesive-backed foam tape in the weatherstripping products section of your local building center.

As the overlapping roof panels are installed and sealed, attach the roof cap sections at the roof ridge to cover the panel overlaps. Seal as directed. *Note:* Completing one section at a time allows you to access subsequent sections from below so that you don't risk damaging the roof.

Attach the peak caps to cover the openings at the ends of the roof cap and then install the roof trim pieces at the bottoms of the roof panels, tucking the flanges or tabs into the roof as directed. Install a plywood floor, according to manufacturer instructions.

Assemble the doors, paying close attention to right/left differences on double doors. Attach hinges for swinging doors and rollers for sliding doors.

Install door tracks and door roller hardware on the floor as directed and then install the doors according to the manufacturer's instructions. Test the action of the doors and make adjustments so the doors roll or swing smoothly and are aligned properly.

Post-and-Board Fence

12

Post-and-board fences include an endless variety of simple designs in which widely spaced square or round posts support several horizontal boards. This type of fence has been around since the early 1700s, remaining popular for its efficient use of lumber and land and its refined appearance.

The post-and-board is still a great design today. Even in a contemporary suburban setting, a classic, white three- or four-board fence evokes the stately elegance of a horse farm or the welcoming, down-home feel of a farmhouse fence bordering a country lane.

Another desirable quality of post-and-board fencing is its ease in conforming to slopes and rolling ground. In fact, it often looks best when the fence rises and dips with ground contours. Of course, you can also build the fence so it's level across the top by trimming the posts along a level line. Traditional agricultural versions of post-and-board fences typically include three to five boards spaced evenly apart or as needed to contain livestock. If you like the look of widely spaced boards but need a more complete barrier for pets, cover the back side of the fence with galvanized wire fencing, which is relatively unnoticeable behind the bold lines of the fence boards. You can also use the basic post-and-board structure to create any number of custom designs. The fence styles shown in the following pages are just a sampling of what you can build using the basic construction technique for post-and-board fences.

TOOLS AND MATERIALS

Mason's string	Combination square
Line level	Lumber (1 × 6, 1 × 4, 2 × 6, 1 × 3)
Circular saw	Deck screws 2," 2½," and 3½"
Speed square	8d galvanized nails
Clamps	Work gloves
4 × 4 posts	Pencil
Finishing materials	
Bar clamps	
Chisel	
Primer paint or stain	
3" stainless-steel screws	
Post levels	

A low post-and-board fence, like traditional picket fencing, is both decorative and functional, creating a modest enclosure without blocking views. The same basic fence made taller and with tighter board spacing becomes an attractive privacy screen or security fence.

Building a Classic Post-and-Board Fence

Set the posts in concrete, following the desired spacing. Laying out the posts at 96" on center allows for efficient use of lumber. For smaller boards, such as 1 × 4s and smaller, set posts closer together for better rigidity.

Trim and shape the posts with a circular saw. For a contoured fence, measure up from the ground and mark the post height according to your plan (post height shown here is 36"). For a level fence, mark the post heights with a level string. If desired, cut a 45° chamfer on the post tops using a speed square to ensure straight cuts. Prime and paint (or stain and seal) the posts.

Mark the board locations by measuring down from the top of each post and making a mark representing the top edge of each board. The traditional 3-board design employs even spacing between boards. Use a speed square to draw a line across the front faces of the posts at each height mark. Mark the post centers on alternate posts using a combination square or speed square and pencil. For strength, it's best to stagger the boards so that butted end joints occur at every other post (this requires 16-ft. boards for posts set 8-ft. apart). The centerlines represent the location of each butted joint.

Install 1 × 6 boards. Measure and mark each board for length, and then cut it to size. Clamp the board to the posts, following the height and center marks. Drill pilot holes and fasten each board end with three 2½" deck screws or 8d galvanized box nails. Use three fasteners where long boards pass over posts as well.

Mark for mitered butt joints at changes in elevation. To mark the miters on contoured fences, draw long centerlines onto the posts. Position an uncut board over the posts at the proper height, and then mark where the top and bottom edges meet the centerline. Connect the marks to create the cutting line, and make the cut. *Note:* The mating board must have the same angle for a symmetrical joint.

Building a Notched-Post Fence

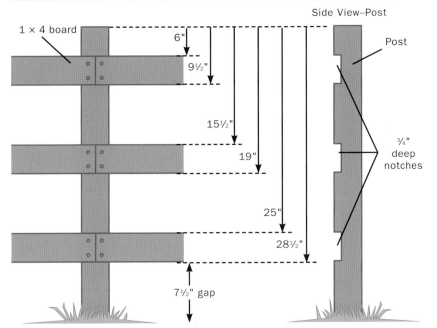

1 × 4 board

Side View–Post

6"

9½"

15½"

19"

25"

28½"

Post

¾" deep notches

7½" gap

The notched-post fence presents a slight variation on the standard face-mounted fence design. Here, each run of boards is let into a notch in the posts so the boards install flush with the post faces. This design offers a cleaner look and adds strength overall to the fence. In this example, the boards are 1 × 4s so the posts are set 6 ft. on center; 1 × 6 or 2 × 6 boards would allow for wider spacing (8 ft.). *Note:* Because the notches must be precisely aligned between posts, the posts are set and braced before the concrete is added. Alternatively, you can complete the post installation and then mark the notches with a string and cut each one with the posts in place.

Cut and mark the posts. Cut the 4 × 4 posts to length at 66". Clamp the posts together with their ends aligned, and mark the notches at 6, 9½, 15½, 19, 25, and 28½" down from the top ends.

Create the notches. Make a series of parallel cuts between the notch marks using a circular saw with the blade depth set at ¾". Clean out the waste and smooth the bases of the notches with a chisel.

Install the posts and boards. Set the posts in their holes and brace them in place using a level string to align the notches. Secure the posts with concrete. Prefinish all fence parts. Install the 1 × 4 boards with 2" deck screws (driven through pilot holes) so their ends meet at the middle of each post.

Building a Capped Post-and-Board Fence

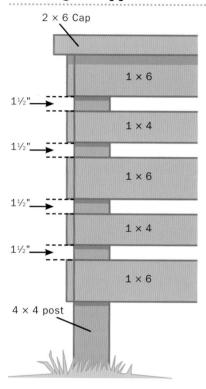

2 × 6 Cap

1 × 6

1½"→

1 × 4

1½"→

1 × 6

1½"→

1 × 4

1½"→

1 × 6

4 × 4 post

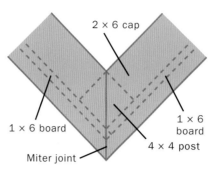

2 × 6 cap

1 × 6 board

1 × 6 board

4 × 4 post

Miter joint

Top View–Detail

A cap rail adds a finished look to a low post-and-board fence. This fence design includes a 2 × 6 cap rail and an infill made of alternating 1 × 4 and 1 × 6 boards for a decorative pattern and a somewhat more enclosed feel than you get with a basic 3-board fence. The cap pieces are mitered over the corner posts. Where cap boards are joined together over long runs of fence, they should meet at a scarf joint—made with opposing 30 or 45° bevels cut into the end of each board. All scarf and miter joints should occur over the center of a post.

Install and mark the posts. Set the 4 × 4 posts in concrete with 72" on-center spacing. Trim the post tops so they are level with one another and approximately 36" above grade. Prefinish all fence parts. Use a square and pencil to mark a vertical centerline on each post where the board ends will butt together.

Install the boards. For each infill bay, cut two 1 × 4s and three 1 × 6s to length. Working from the top of the posts down, fasten the boards with 2½" deck screws driven through pilot holes. Use a 1½"-thick spacer (such as a 2 × 4 laid flat) to ensure even spacing between boards.

Add the cap rail. Cut the cap boards so they will install flush with the inside faces and corners of the posts; this creates a 1¼" overhang beyond the boards on the front side of the fence. Fasten the cap pieces to the posts with 3½" deck screws driven through pilot holes.

Building a Modern Post-and-Board Privacy Fence

This beautiful, modern-style post-and-board fence is made with pressure-treated 4 × 4 posts and clear cedar 1 × 3, 1 × 4, and 1 × 6 boards. To ensure quality and color consistency, it's a good idea to hand-pick the lumber, and choose S4S (surfaced on four sides) for a smooth, sleek look. Alternative materials include clear redwood, ipé, and other rot-resistant species. A high-quality, UV-resistant finish is critical to preserve the wood's natural coloring for as long as possible.

Install the posts, spacing them 60" on-center or as desired. Mark the tops of the posts with a level line, and trim them at 72" above grade. *Note:* This fence design is best suited to level ground. Cut the fence boards to length. If desired, you can rip down wider stock for custom board widths (but you'll have to sand off any saw marks for a finished look).

Fasten the boards to the post faces using 2½" deck screws or 8d galvanized box nails driven through pilot holes. Work from the top down, and use ⅞"-thick wood spacers to ensure accurate spacing.

Add the battens to cover the board ends and hide the posts. Use 1 × 4 boards for the infill posts and 1 × 6s for the corner posts. Rip ¾" from the edge of one corner batten so the assembly is the same width on both sides. Fasten the battens to the posts with 3" stainless-steel screws (other screw materials can discolor the wood).

Garden Aids

In many ways, the self-sufficient home revolves around the garden. Growing and harvesting your own produce enables you to declare some measure of independence from the corporate food chain. It also allows you control what goes into what you grow, meaning that you'll eat less pesticides, chemicals from processed fertilizer, and other contaminants. And don't forget the money you'll save by raising your own organic produce.

But self-sufficient gardening is something more as well. It's the chance to get involved with your food and truly "get back to the land." There is nothing quite like a few sore muscles and the knowledge that at the end of a day of gardening, you've done simple, good work. You soak up sunshine, get the most wholesome form of exercise you can get, and achieve something tangible and positive. You could hardly ask for a more rewarding outdoor activity.

Of course, gardening involves much more than simply digging in the dirt and dropping a seed in a hole. In fact, it starts with that dirt. Healthy soil will be the foundation of all you do in the garden, and without it, your labor is likely to be much less productive. That's why building a Two-Bin Composter like the one on page 97, or a Soil Sifter like the one on page 111, leads in a straight to more healthy and productive garden. Other amenities, like a Vermiculture Bin (page 103) are less directly related to what you grow, but can still offer immense help to your efforts.

Beyond how they will benefit your garden, these structures are also interesting and rewarding projects to build. Everything in this section is fairly easy to construct, requiring little in the way of complicated tools and techniques. Basically, if you know how to operate a saw and use a drill, you'll be able to execute all of the projects that follow. Once you build them, your garden will thank you season after season, with edible gifts.

Clothesline Trellis

13

Modifying or repurposing a clothesline support to serve as a trellis is not a new idea, but it's certainly a good one. It's also kind of a head-slapper, as in, "Why didn't I think of that?" After all, you've got this tall, sturdy, utilitarian structure taking up space in a sunny spot that's easy to reach from the house … so why not grow some plants on it?

If you don't already have a clothesline support or two that you can be turned into a trellis, you can build this one from scratch. The construction is easier than it looks. All of the beams and uprights are joined with special timber screws, so there's no complex or custom-fit joinery. And you can build the entire trellis in your shop or garage, then dig a couple of holes and get it set up in one go.

The basic structure of the trellis is inspired by the Torii, a traditional Japanese gateway to a shrine or other sacred place. The overhanging top beam, or lintel, is a characteristic feature for this type of structure and in this case can be used to support hanging plants or wind chimes or simply be left as is for a clean look. The vertical spindles in the center of the trellis are made with 1½-inch-square pressure-treated stock. (You can also use cedar or redwood.) They're offset from one another in an alternating pattern for a subtle decorative effect. You can change the spacing of the spindles as needed to suit your plants, or even use a different material, such round spindles, wire or string.

This trellis makes a great garden feature that looks good year-round and can serve as a focal point or a divider between landscape zones. You can build just one trellis and run the clotheslines between the trellis and a fence, your house or garage, or a garden shed or other outbuilding.

A trellis such as this is not only very attractive all in it's own right, it also serves two functional roles—holding up plants and holding up laundry!

Building a Clothesline Trellis

Key	No.	Part	Dimension	Material*
A	2	Post	3½ x 3½" x 10 ft.	4 x 4
B	1	Lintel	3½ x 3½ x 81"	4 x 4
C	2	Cross Beam	3½ x 3½ x 47"	4 x 4
D	7	Spindle	1½" x 1½ x 47½"	2 x 2
E	1	Spreader	3½" x 3½ x 8½"	4 x 4

*All lumber can be pressure-treated or all-heart cedar or redwood or other naturally rot-resistant wood.

TOOLS AND MATERIALS

Miter saw
Cordless drill and bits
Nail set
Tongue-and-groove pliers or adjustable wrench
Posthole digger
6" self-drilling timber screws (24)
2" exterior finish nails
⅜ x 2¾" galvanized or stainless-steel
   screw eyes or screw hooks
   (4, with lag-screw threads)
Gravel

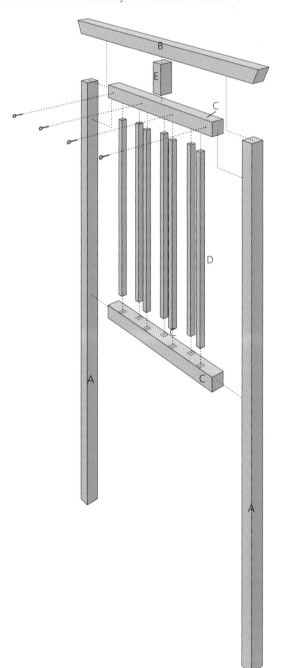

Using a miter saw or circular saw, cut both ends of the cross beams square. Cut the ends of the lintel at 30°. Cut the top end of each 10-ft. post to ensure a clean, square cut with no splits; the bottom end will be buried at least 3 ft. deep, so overall length isn't critical.

Mark the inside faces of the two posts for the cross beam locations, using a square to draw layout lines across the post faces. Mark the underside of the lintel in the same way; it is centered over the long posts, while the center post is centered on the lintel.

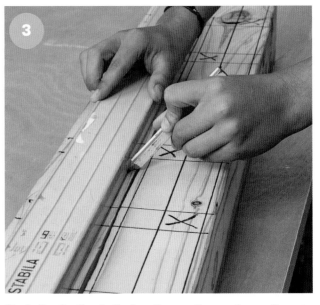

Mark the 2 x 2 spindle locations on the cross beams. For more contrast, you can offset the locations – but remember to mark the opposing sides of the cross beam as mirror images. Here the spindles are placed ¼" in from the edges and spaced 4⅝" apart.

(continued)

Test-fit the frame assembly on a flat work surface. Fasten the cross beams to the posts with two 6" self-drilling timber screws at each joint. You may need to drill pilot holes if the screws are difficult to drive. Drive the screws with either a drill or an impact driver and a hex-type nut driver or other bit (special bits often come with boxes of timber screws). If your 4 × 4s are well-dried, you can attach the lintel now; if not, save some back strain and bolt it on after the posts are upright.

Dig two holes at least 3 ft. deep for the posts. Shovel a few inches of gravel into each hole, then tip the whole assembly in (use a helper—wet treated wood is heavy). Plumb and brace the posts with 1 × 2s.

Check that the cross beams are level. To raise one side, simply add a little gravel under the post. Fill the post holes with alternating layers of soil and gravel. Or you can fill the holes with concrete. Check level and plumb as you fill the holes. Tamp the dirt and gravel so that the posts are firmly locked in place.

Set the lintel in position, aligning it with the marks made earlier, then fasten it in place with timber screws.

Cut the 2 × 2s to fit tightly, then fasten with predrilled 6d casing nails or a pneumatic nailer. Use two nails at each end.

Clotheslines for Climbers

Here are a few tips for planning and setting up a decorative and highly functional clothesline system:

· When the leaves are out, the trellis can create a nice a shady spot for a bench on the side opposite the clotheslines.

· A typical load of laundry needs about 35 linear feet of clothesline and weighs about 15 to 18 pounds after spinning in the washing machine. Therefore, running three or four 12 to 15-foot lines each strikes a good balance for minimizing sag on the loaded lines while providing plenty of room for hanging.

· Clothesline materials include solid-metal wire, stranded wire or cable, plastic-coated cable, and traditional clothesline rope. Wire lines last longer and stretch less than rope, but many clothesline devotees prefer rope for its natural look and feel as well as its thickness and texture, which make it ideal for gripping fabric and clothespins.

· Pulleys allow you to hang and retrieve clothes from one standing position. Metal pulleys are strong and won't break down with UV exposure (like plastic wheels will), but make sure all metal parts are rust-resistant (stainless steel is best).

· Turnbuckles provide means for tensioning wire lines without having to restring or reclamp them. Tighten rope lines by simply retying them, or you can add a hook and a trampoline spring to maintain tension and make it easy to remove the line without untying it.

Two-bin Composter

14

When it's time to get serious about composting, a multiple-bin system is the way to go. They're designed to produce a large volume of compost in a short time. The idea is to develop a nice, big heap in one bin, then start turning it over by shoveling it into the neighboring bin, then back to the first bin, and so on. Turning greatly speeds decomposition (plus, it gives you a little exercise in the process). Depending on the compost materials, turning is recommended every 5 to 10 days. A two-bin composter lets you flip the heap back and forth between bins until the compost is ready, then you can store it one bin and use the other bin to start building the next heap.

This design facilitates turning with its removable divider between the bins. Simply slide the divider up and out of the way for easy shoveling. The front sides of the bins are full-width gates, providing easy access to the bins for moving material in or out.

But perhaps the best feature of this composter has nothing to do with production; it's all about appearances. As much as self-sufficient homeowners and gardeners love the idea of composting, few can honestly say they like the look of a compost heap. (And the aesthetics of plastic barrels or trashcan composters need no further criticism.) You may not see a lot of bin-type composters with cedar pickets, decorative posts, and traditional gates, but what would you rather look at: a pile of rotting garbage or a well-built picket fence?

TIP

Three-peat Enough

A three-bin system uses the same idea as a two-bin composter, but the additional bin helps make the process even more continuous. Once your heap is ready, flip it into bin two and use bins two and three for turning. This leaves bin one open for compiling the next heap. You can easily adapt this two-bin composter design to create a three-bin version. Just extend the overall length by a third, and create another center divider and gate. The two stringers along the backside of the structure can be cut from 12-foot 2 x 4s.

Composting is key in a truly self-sufficient garden, and the only thing better than an active composting bin, is a doubly active bin.

Building a Two-Bin Composter

CUTTING LIST

Key	No.	Part	Dimension	Material*
A	6	Posts	3½ x 3½ x 60 "	4 x 4 PT pine
B	49	Pickets	¾ x 3½ x 36 "	1 x 4 PT pine
C	2	Rear rail	1½ x 3½ x 93 "	2 x 4 PT pine
D	4	Side rail	1½ x 3½ x 45 "	2 x 4 PT pine
E	4	Hinge blocks	1½ x 3½ x 5 "	2 x 4 PT pine
F	4	Gate rails	1½ x 3½ x 39¼ "	2 x 4 PT pine
G	2	Latch block	1½ x 3½ x 3½ "	2 x 4 PT pine
H	4	Divider panel stops	1½ x 1½ x 30 "	2 x 2 PT pine
J	2	Divider rail	1½ x 3½ x 34 "	2 x 4 PT pine

*Use pressure-treated lumber rated for ground contact or all-heart cedar, redwood, or other naturally rot-resistant species.

TOOLS AND MATERIALS

Hand maul
4 ft. level
Posthole digger
Tamper
Miter saw
Cordless drill and bits
Gravel
Deck Screws 1⅝," 3½"
Exterior-grade construction adhesive
½ x ½" galvanized hardware cloth with staples (optional)
(4) 3½ gate hinges with screws
(2) Gate latches with screws
4 x 4 post caps (optional)

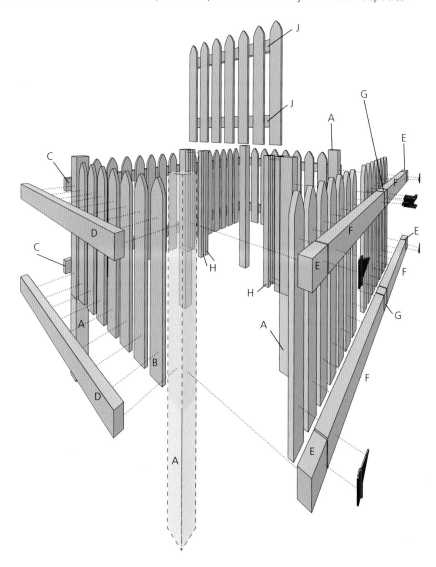

Choose a flat, level site at least 6 × 10 ft. that allows for movement in front of the bins. Cut the back rails and posts to length, then lay them out on a flat surface. Square the assembly by making sure the diagonals are equal. Fasten the rails to the posts with 3½" deck screws.

Set the assembled back wall in place, then mark the hole locations with chalk or a shovel. Dig holes 8" in diameter by 24" deep at each post location.

Plumb and level the posts using wood braces. Fill the holes with gravel and dirt. The bottom rails should be roughly 6" to 8" above ground level.

(continued)

Dig holes for the front posts, using a framing square and a side rail (or the 3-4-5 method) to locate the correct position. Put the posts in and fasten the top rail to both front and rear posts to help hold the front post plumb and level. Fill the holes with alternating layers of gravel and dirt and attach the bottom rails. Position the center post so that it's the same distance from the corner posts and in line with both of them.

At the front corner posts and front center post, measure and cut six short 2 × 4s to cover the front faces of the posts (5" long at the corners and 3½" at the center). These continue the runs of the stringers and will serve as mounting blocks for the gate hinges and latches. Install the blocks as you did with the rear stringers, but predrill and countersink all screw holes to avoid cracking the short pieces of wood.

Install the pickets along the back and sides with 1⅝" deck screws. Keep the pickets 1½" to 2" above the ground to prevent rot. The fastest way to install the pickets is to make spacer blocks. For this design, the seven pickets on the sides were spaced 1⅝" apart and the back and front pickets were spaced 1⅞" apart. To find the spacing for a different size bin, just subtract the total width of seven pickets (or however many you use) from the distance between the posts, then divide the result by 8 (the number of spaces between pickets). Use a 5"-high block of wood at the top to quickly establish the height for each picket.

Begin constructing the gates. Set the rails on your work surface so they are parallel and spaced the same distance apart as the bin stringers. Space the pickets 1⅞" apart like the back wall, but start from the center—line up the center of the first picket with the center of the rail, then work to each side so you end up with roughly 1⅞" between the last picket and the post. Fasten the pickets to the rails with 1⅝" screws and construction adhesive. The construction adhesive helps prevent the gate from sagging over time. Check the assembly for square as you work.

Clamp or screw a straight piece of wood across the three front posts to support the gates while the hinges and latches are attached. Hang the gates using gate hinges—both gates open out and away from the center post. Install latch hardware for each gate so it locks closed at the center post.

Cut the four stops for the sliding divider panel from 2 × 2s. Make marks at 1¼" in from the edges on both posts. Install the 2 × 2 stops against these lines with predrilled 3½" screws, creating a 1" slot at the center. The outside edges of the stops will overhang the edges of the posts by about ¼".

> ### TIP
> ### Upgrades
>
> Add a touch of beauty to your compost bin by attaching a decorative post cap to the top of each 4 x 4 post. You can find a wide variety at home centers or online. You also may want to fasten a 2-ft. wide strip of ½" hardware cloth down to the ground around the inside of the composter to help keep all the compost inside the bin.

Build the divider panel using the same construction techniques used for the gates, but extend the outside pickets beyond the 2 × 4 rails so they fit into the channels between the stops. Space the pickets 2⅛" apart. The total width of the panel should be about ½" narrower than the distance between the posts so that the panel can slide in and out without binding. To keep the divider panel at the same height as the rest of the enclosure, screw in a small wood stop or a few screws near the bottom of the slot.

Basement Vermiculture Bin

If you're new to vermiculture, this multi-bin unit is a great way to enter the wonderful world of worm poop. And if you've been working with a simple one-bin system in a plastic storage container, you're probably ready to take your composting to another level—or how about three levels? Actually, you can have as many levels as you like; they're all interchangeable and very easy to build. Just add bins as needed to increase production.

Multi-bin, or flow-through, vermiculture systems offer a few advantages over single-compartment composters. The main benefit is that flow-through systems allow you to harvest the compost without having to sift through the bin, or to dump out everything then put back the worms, bedding, and incomplete compost material. Harvesting is much easier for you and also less disruptive to the worms, helping them stay in "production" mode. The stacked design of vertical flow-through systems makes these composters space-efficient, an obvious plus when composting indoors.

The process couldn't be simpler: Fill the upper bins with worms and compost material. As the worms eat the material, their castings (also known as *vermicompost*) fall through to the bottom bin. To harvest the compost, lift off the upper bins and empty the bottom level. Then reset the stack so the middle bin is now on the bottom, and the empty bottom bin is now on top; fill this bin with new material to keep the process going. The worms will travel up through the bins as they exhaust their food sources, so you never have to move more than a few stragglers at harvest time.

Vermiculture creates moisture (called leachate), which you'll have to catch in a tray or baking pan. You can set the stack of bins right into a pan, using blocks to ensure airflow, or you can build a handy base that supports the bins and provides a space for a tray to slide underneath (see Building the Optional Base, right). Speaking of moisture, if you're used to composting with a plastic tub, you'll find that an open wood system like this dries out more quickly than a plastic container, so be sure to check the moisture level regularly and mist the compost material with a spray bottle and non-chlorinated water as needed.

Building the Optional Base

The base is constructed much like the bin frames, with two ends fitting between two sides. Cut two 2 x 6 sides to 23½" long and two ends to 20½." Make a side cutout in the top edge of each 2 x 6, using a jigsaw. The cutouts allow you to grab the 1x2 edging to lift off the bins. Assemble the frame with 3" deck screws. Slide a sheet pan or plastic tray inside the base to collect leachate.

Make the most of worm castings (better known as poop), by setting up your own worm bin in the corner of a basement.

Building a Basement Vermiculture Bin

CUTTING LIST

Key	No.	Part	Dimension	Material
A	6	End	¾ x 3½ x 18½"	1 x 4 clear pine or cedar
B	6	Side	¾ x 3½ x 20"	1 x 4 clear pine or cedar
C	6	End edging	¾ x 1½ x 20"	1 x 2 clear pine or cedar
D	6	Side edging	¾ x 1½ x 21½"	1 x 2 clear pine or cedar
E	1	Lid	¾ x 22 x 22"	¾" plywood
F	1	Handle	¾ x 1½ x 6"	1 x 2 clear pine or cedar

TOOLS AND MATERIALS

Miter saw or circular saw
Cordless drill and bits
Wire cutters
Deck screws 1¼, 1, 2, 3"
Waterproof wood glue
Galvanized hardware
  cloth with ¼" grid
  (20 x 60" min.)
¾" washer-head wood
  screws
Handle with screws
Drip tray and blocks
  (as applicable)

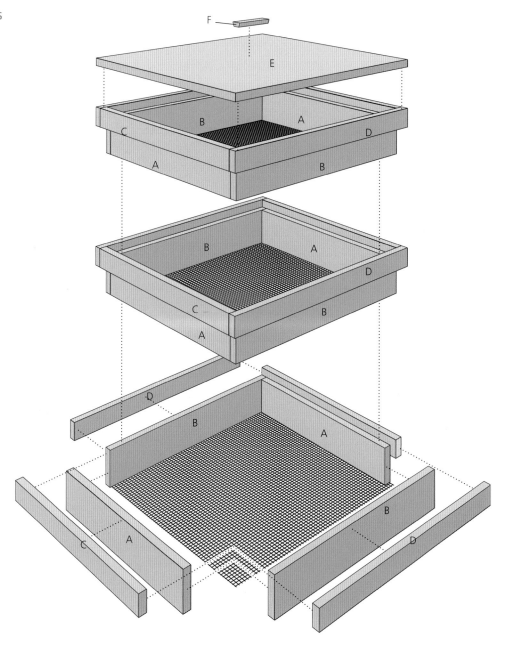

Assemble each bin frame by fitting the ends between the sides so all edges are flush. Drill pilot holes for three screws at each joint. Apply glue and fasten the joints with 2" deck screws. Use a square or measure diagonally between opposing corners to ensure the frame is square. Let the glue dry as directed.

Measure the outside dimensions of each assembled frame and cut a piece of hardware cloth ¼" smaller than the frame's width and length. Center the mesh over the frame, leaving a ⅛" margin along all edges. Fasten the mesh to the frame edges with ¾" washer-head screws spaced about 4" apart.

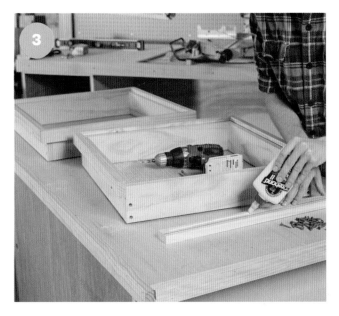

Add the 1 x 2 edging that serves as handles and ledges so that the bins can nest into one another. Position the edging against one side so the top is ½" above the frame's top edge, and the edging is flush with the frame ends. Drill pilot holes, apply glue, and fasten the edging to the frame with 1¼" deck screws. Install the rest of the edging in the same fashion.

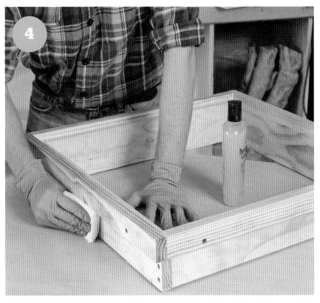

Sand the edges of the lid as necessary and add a handle to the center of the panel. *Note:* Oil the wood parts of your bins to add moisture protection and to help keep the wood from absorbing liquids from the compost. Use a food-grade oil, such as walnut oil, and apply as directed.

(continued)

Potato-Growing Box

16

Potatoes have a funny way of growing. They start under soil, like most plants, but as their shoots reach up through the soil toward the sun, they develop roots that extend horizontally from the main taproot, ultimately yielding fruit. If you leave the emerged foliage alone, each plant will grow one batch of potatoes, but if you cover some of the foliage with soil, more roots will grow underground, yielding more fruit for harvest.

This space-efficient method of "vertical gardening" is made possible with a potato box: You plant your seed potatoes inside a single level, or course, of the box, covering them with soft soil or mulch. When the plants grow to a height of 8 to 12-inches above the soil, you add another layer to the box and cover about one-third of the plants' height with soil; the buried portions of foliage will form new lateral roots as the plant continues its upward climb. Repeat the process until harvest time, when you simply disassemble the box to get to your spuds.

This potato-box design includes two special features that facilitate assembly and disassembly, as well as off-season storage. The box sides are held together with half-lap joints, so no fasteners are needed for assembly. The boards on opposing sides of the course have 2 × 2 cleats that extend down to interlock with the course below to prevent shifting. At harvest, the box quickly disassembles without tools or digging, and the boards stack neatly for storage.

TIP

Growing Superlative Spuds

• Start with disease-free "seed potatoes" purchased from a garden center or seed store.
• Proper watering is key to a healthy, nice-looking crop: Maintain even moisture levels and monitor the box carefully because container-grown potatoes can dry out relatively quickly.
• Prevent disease contamination by moving your potato box to a new location each year and use new soil for each growing season.
• In climates with frost, harvest potatoes after frost kills the exposed foliage. In climates without frost, cut off the plants and let the potatoes sit for 1½ to 2 weeks before harvesting.
• Check with a local extension office or master gardener for potato growing and storage tips specific to your area, as well as recommendations for potato varieties that thrive in the local climate.

Growing a wealth of potatoes can be easy as long as you have the right container. Look no further for the new garden home of your next starchy crop.

Building a Potato-Growing Box

Key	No.	Part	Dimension	Material
A	16	Box side	1½ x 5½ x 29½"	2 x 6
B	16	Cleat	1½ x 1½ x 5"	2 x 2

*All-heartwood redwood or cedar or other naturally rot-resistant lumber is recommended. Avoid cupped boards.

TOOLS AND MATERIALS

Table saw or circular saw
Drill
2½" deck screws
Mallet
Chisel

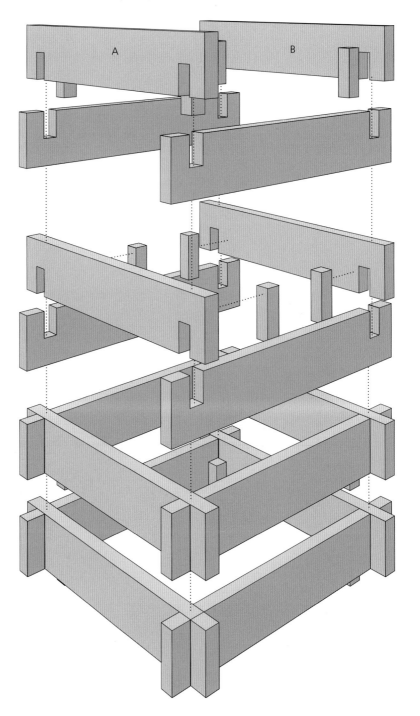

Cut the sides for the box carefully. All the pieces need to be exactly the same dimensions and the ends perfectly square. Lay out the half-lap notches on two of the boards as shown, making each 1⁹⁄₁₆" wide. Screw a straight board to the sliding miter gauge to keep the sides straight as you push them through. The depth of each notch is exactly half of the board's width, so measure the boards and adjust the depth as needed. Align and clamp the boards to the miter gauge. Make the first cut at 2" from the end, then slide the boards over 1⁹⁄₁₆" and make the second cut. (You can also use a circular saw or a jigsaw to make these cuts.)

Break off the waste material and clean up the bottom of the notch with a sharp chisel. Check the fit. If everything looks good, cut the rest of the boards on the table saw. If you're using a circular saw, trace the notches onto the remaining boards with a sharp pencil, then cut out all of the remaining notches. Note: Only the bottom layer of boards has to be the exact same depth. If it's a little deep, you can drive a screw in at the base and turn it in or out to make the top edges level.

Use a square to mark positioning lines for the cleats on each board, marking the lines just to the inside of each notch. These represent the outside faces of the 2 × 2 cleats. Mark a vertical line 3" above the base of each notch; this represents the top end of each cleat. Install the cleats by drilling countersunk pilot holes and fastening the cleats to the boards with pairs of 2½" deck screws. Note: For the bottom course of the box, you can omit the cleats, if desired, or you can make longer cleats with pointed ends to help anchor the box to the ground.

Test-fit the parts by assembling the entire box. Use a framing square or measure diagonally between opposing corners of the box frame to make sure the frame is square. Plant your seed potatoes about 4 to 8" deep and cover with soil or mulch. As the plants spring out of the ground, add more soil and additional courses until the box is complete.

Soil Sifter

17

Sifting your soil is an excellent way to refine the foundation of your garden. The basic idea is to sift the soil through a screen much as you would sift ingredients for baking. Sifting "cleans" the soil, removing large organic objects such as rocks and debris like broken glass. The process improves the texture of the soil, loosening it to allow for better water and air penetration. It can also remove old weed rhizomes—root systems that could grow new colonies of weeds. The benefits include improved drainage and moisture retention so that your plants' roots are more likely to get the water they need without becoming waterlogged or rotting.

You can take the opportunity of sifting your soil to blend in amendments such as compost, manure, or other nutritional additions. It's a great way to create a premium top soil that will get your garden off to a great start—and keep it growing strong throughout the season.

Sifting soil can be done with nothing more than a sturdy, thick mesh screen held by the edges. But if your garden is like most, you'll be faced with sifting quite a bit of soil and a simple hand-held screen will be quite laborious to use. That's why the design of the sifter described in the pages that follow is a bit more sophisticated. It uses a sifting box equipped with wheels, and this box sits in a frame. You sift the soil by rolling the box back and forth within the frame, saving a lot of energy, effort, and sore backs. If you want to make the rig even handier and easier to store, add handles to both the sifting box and frame.

The sifting frame has been sized to fit perfectly over a standard wheelbarrow. But if you are using another container to catch the sifted soil, or if your wheelbarrow is a different size, adjust the measurements to suit. This could even be used over an empty garbage can or barrel. Once you've constructed the sifter, sift soil for your whole garden, container plants, or anywhere you want clean, effective top soil. Your plants will thank you.

Sifting soil is largely a lost craft in the garden, but one that can go far toward improving your soil and making your plants grow as healthy as possible.

Building a Soil Sifter

CUTTING LIST

Key	No.	Part	Dimension	Material
A	2	Frame Stile	¾ x 2½ x 35"	1 x 3
B	2	Frame Rail	1½ x 3½ x 30"	2 x 4
C	2	Frame Guide	¾ x ¾ x 35"	¾ x ¾
D	2	Box Side	1½ x 3½ x 25"	2 x 4
E	2	Box End	1½ x 3½ x 28"	2 x 4

TOOLS AND MATERIALS

(4) 1" rigid casters (uni-directional)
¼" or ½" galvanized screen
Cordless drill and bits
1¼" washer head screws
   (also known as lath screws)
2½" deck screws
1¼" wood screws
1½" wide metal angle
¾" x #8 pan head screws

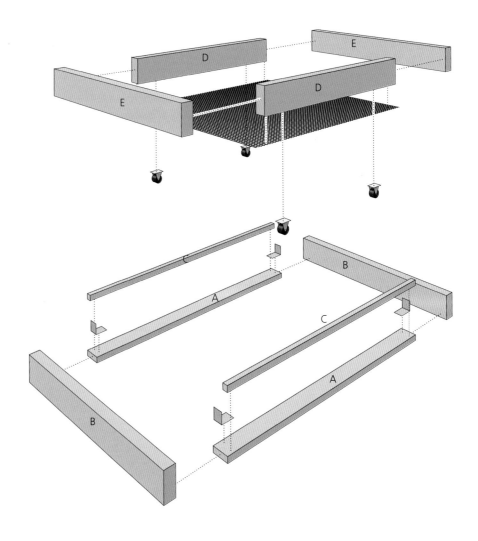

Drill pilot holes through the frame guides and into the 1 × 3 frame stiles. Screw the guides to the stile with 1¼" wood screws, ensuring that the guides are aligned along one edge of each stile. These guides will serve as tracks for the soil-sifting box.

Join the frame rails to the stiles with a metal angle at each corner.

Screw the sifting box ends to the box sides with 2½" deck screws. Cut the screen ¼" less than the size of the box. Screw it to one side with washer head screws, then stretch it tightly and screw it to the opposite side. Use at least 4 screws per side.

Screw the casters to the back and front ends of each box side so that the wheels face toward the ends.

Octagon Strawberry Planter and Cover

18

Growing strawberries is equally popular among gardeners and animals. Gardeners love them because they grow like weeds in almost any climate, and there's no fruit better than a freshly picked organic strawberry. Animals like them for that second reason. The bright, red color and sweet fragrance of ripening strawberries is a siren song to every squirrel and other varmint within a mile radius, it seems. If you've grown strawberries in an open garden patch, you also know that the plants tend to multiply like rabbits, quickly taking over the patch if not controlled.

This easy-to-build planter covers you on both fronts. The wood frame attractively contains the plants while keeping them all within easy reach, and the lightweight mesh cover critter-proofs your crop in seconds. The planter looks best without the cover, so you can leave it off while the fruit is still green. Just be sure to keep the cover in place once the strawberries start to ripen (you can be sure the birds and other critters are watching … and waiting).

Building the planter frame is a cinch with a power miter saw, but you can also use a circular saw or even a handsaw and a tall miter box. Most miter saws will cut a 2 × 4 set on-edge; for larger lumber, you'll need a 12-inch miter saw or a sliding compound miter saw, which can make the miter cuts while the wood is flat on the saw table.

The planter as shown is 69 inches wide. If desired, you can modify the size simply by cutting shorter or longer pieces; they're all the same size and all have their ends cut at 22½°. You can even change the shape of the planter—to create a hexagon or decagon, for example. The math is simple: To determine the angle cuts, simply double the number of sides and divide that number into 360. For example, a hexagon has six sides; therefore: $360 \div 12 = 30$. Make each end cut at 30° and you'll have a perfect hexagon. The mesh cover is custom-fit to the planter size. You'll find the bird netting we used for a cover at nurseries and home centers.

Option for Off-Season Storage

Leave off the glue and use metal strapping and screws on two of the wood joints so that you can disassemble the planter for winter. Choose any two opposing corner joints (dividing the octagonal frame in half) and join the wood members with metal straps, or ties, and 1½" galvanized screws. The metal straps are designed for structural framing connections and are sold at home centers. Check the building materials department for deck-framing connectors.

Strawberries are some of the most popular fruits grown in the home garden. This octagonal planter provides for as much as you can grow, eat, make into jam or put up.

Building an Octagon Strawberry Planter and Cover

CUTTING LIST

Key	No.	Part	Dimension	Material*
A	8	Planter side	1½ x 3½ x 28½"	2 x 4
B	4	Cover support	¼ x ¾ x 72"	Screen molding

*All-heart cedar or redwood or other naturally rot-resistant wood species is recommended.

TOOLS AND MATERIALS

Miter saw
Cordless drill and bits
Waterproof wood glue

3" deck screws
Bird block netting
Speed square

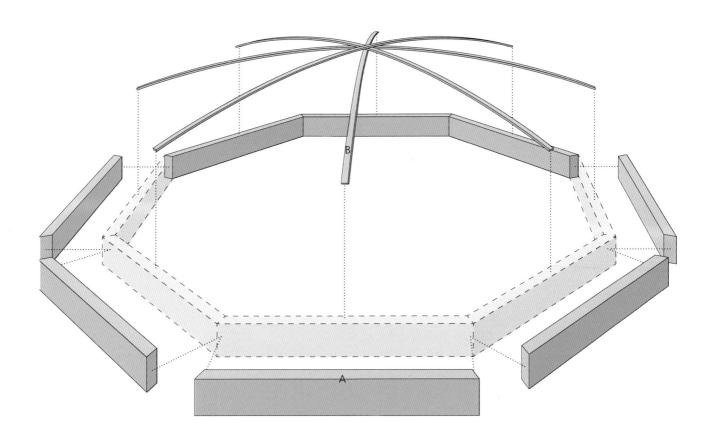

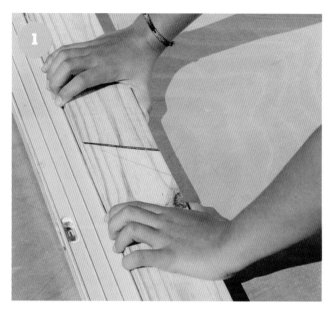

Set up your miter saw and run some test cuts to make sure the angle setting is accurate. Cut two pieces of scrap 2 x 4 at 22½°. Fit the pieces together end to end and check the assembly with a straight edge; the pieces should be perfectly straight. (If you're using a circular saw, cut test pieces with the saw blade tilted at 22½°.)

Use a stop block setup to ensure that all pieces are precisely the same length. This speeds your work and ensures the joints will fit tightly. For this roughly 6-ft.-wide planter, each piece is 28½" long, measuring between the long points of the two angled ends. To make the cuts, leave the miter saw set on one side and just flip the board over for each successive cut.

Drill pilot holes through one frame piece and into its mating piece, starting the hole about ⅞" from the pointed end of the first piece. Angle the hole slightly toward the inside of the joint (what will be the inside of the assembled frame). This gives the screws a little bit of cross-grain penetration, helping them hold better than if they were perfectly parallel to the grain of the mating piece.

Apply glue and fasten each joint with two screws. For extra strength, add a third screw driven from the opposite direction as the first two. *Tip:* Work on a flat surface, such as a garage floor, to help keep the pieces flush at the top and bottom so the entire assembly will be flat.

(continued)

Dig out the grass and soil at least several inches deep and replace it with high quality garden soil mix. Cover the soil with landscape fabric to keep unwanted grass or weeds from growing. Use nails or spikes to hold the fabric in place, then trim it flush with the octagon edges.

Create an arched dome with wooden screen molding. Predrill holes at each end for screws, using a drill bit bigger than the size of the screw. Mark the centers of each 2 × 4. Screw one end in, leaving the screw about ½" out of the wood. Move to the opposite side, arch the wood, and put a screw in on that side, tightening it just enough to hold the end down. Join the frame rails to the stiles with a metal corner at each stile.

Spread an inch or two of mulch over the landcape fabric, then plant the octagon with strawberry plants. Cut slits in the fabric where each plant goes and then work the plant down into the garden soil.

Spread bird netting over the dome. Hold it in place by hooking it on two roundhead screws or small nails on each side. Trim the excess. To take the netting off, wrap one side around a piece of smooth wood or a 6-ft.-long pole and just roll it up. When you want to cover the strawberries in the spring, just hook one side and roll it out again.

Project Detail: Filling Your Strawberry Planter

Strawberries are some of the most popular plants among home gardeners, and for good reason. Put in a little bit of work and diligence, and you'll be rewarded with a bumper crop of incredibly sweet and delicious fruit. Building the octagonal planter in this project is the first step to success—by growing in a raised planter, you control the growing culture and ensure protection for the plants. The next step is the soil.

Fill the planter with loamy soil rich in organic matter, with a pH around 6. Use bagged soil to avoid any problems; strawberries don't grow well in soil that has supported sod, and are susceptible to disease from soils in which peppers, tomatoes, eggplant, and potatoes have grown.

Next, you'll need to decide on the type of strawberries you want to plant (the type available in your local growing zone may influence your decision, so it's best to check catalogs and local nurseries before settling on a specific variety). You'll choose between three different types: June bearing, everbearing and day neutral. June bearing strawberries are the largest and produce all their fruit over a three-week period (this type is further broken down into early, late, or mid-season varieties).

Despite their name, everbearing strawberries don't produce continuous harvests. Instead, most will yield three separate harvests, roughly corresponding to spring, summer, and fall. Day neutral, on the other hand, will grow fruit all through the warm months. Most gardeners—looking to optimize their yields—grow more than one variety. However, everbearing and day neutral are better suited to the confines of a planter or raised bed.

Once you get your plants home, you'll need to plant them correctly. Many novice home gardeners plant their strawberry plants improperly, causing lower yields and even die-off between seasons (if properly cared for, your plants will produce strawberries for four years or more). Plant strawberries after all threat of frost has passed. Always plant on an overcast day, or early in the morning before the sun is bright. The shock of transplanting coupled with bright direct sun can damage strawberry plants.

Each plant should be buried deep enough so that the roots are just barely but completely covered, and the crown is exposed (see below).

This is the proper planting depth for a strawberry plant; notice that no portion of the roots is exposed and that the crown is fully aboveground.

Professionals recommend removing the flowers on June-bearing strawberries when they appear in the first year. When the flowers are removed, the plant puts all its energy into growing strong roots and runners that will result in new plants. This translates to a much larger crop the second year. Nursery pros recommend removing the flowers on everbearing and day neutral varieties until the end of June for the same reason.

Aftercare is important for strawberry plant health. Make sure they are getting six full hours of sun a day. If not, move the planter. Before the next season, cut off old foliage down to the crown each year, and mulch the plants well over winter, to ensure against freezing.

Teepee Trellis

19

Vertical gardening is one of the best ways to produce a large harvest in a modest amount of space. That's why trellises are so popular in gardens and why there are so many different trellis designs. The teepee style shown here is popular among homesteaders of all stripes because it's easy to build, saves space, is adaptable, and costs next to nothing.

The teepee trellis in this project is one of the simplest, including only three legs and connecting wire that creates horizontal surfaces to encourage even more plant growth. We've used widely available 1× cedar legs that you can find at any home center or lumberyard. If you're not fond of square-leg design, you can always substitute dowels or other materials (see page 123 for a rundown of different options). This design is meant to be portable, so that you can use it in different areas of the garden at different times or seasons. It also means that you can store the trellis in a shed or garage over the winter, which will prolong its life. Portability is just one aspect of the amazing adaptability in this type of trellis.

For instance, you can use longer poles to accommodate the greater vegetation of more aggressive growers. Or use more poles, creating a variety of surfaces for your vining plants to exploit. Space them wide apart, leave a large gap on one side so that the mature plants provide a shady refuge for kids, or modify any one of a number of ways that are pretty much only limited to the margins of your imagination.

No matter how you build it, your plants are sure to thrive on a teepee trellis. Although it provides a maximum of vertical growing space, it also allows for ample light penetration and airflow, ensuring against disease and keeping your plants as happy as can be.

A teepee trellis like this is a space-conserving way to grow a large crop of runner beans or other vining vegetable. You can even grow flowering vines up one side for a showstopping garden addition.

TIP

Vertical Plants

There are an amazing variety of plants to grow up a trellis such as this. Some are easy choices, commonly found species that you're likely to find at the local nursery or home centers. But you can also use your teepee trellis for somewhat more unusual choices.

Runner Beans. These are some of the most popular choices for growing on trellises. The plants produce a wealth of tasty beans, and it's easy to put up the extra.

Peas. Peas of all kinds grow like crazy on a teepee trellis. The delicate flower and interesting shoots make them a favorite in a child's garden.

Cucumbers. A smart choice for trellis culture, cucumbers take to vertical living, and insects are less likely to attack the luscious produce on a vertical support.

Tomatoes. Surprised? Don't be. When you grow a tomato plant inside a tomato cage, you're accommodating the plant's need for support. Tie it up to a teepee trellis and the plant will flourish.

Zucchini. This is a teepee trellis favorite, one that grows like crazy with very little maintenance or care. Other squashes are equally enthusiastic about teepee trellis life, but you need to be sure that any plant producing heavier vegetables is properly supported by the teepee's framework material.

Melons. Get your melons up off the ground to do away with mushy, yellow flat spots and to keep them safe from insects. Cantaloupe, honeydew and even watermelon can be grown vertically. Just make sure they are properly supported, and pick them as soon as they are ripe.

Peppers. Peppers of all kinds do extremely well when grown up a teepee trellis.

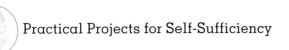

Building a Simple Teepee Trellis

TOOLS AND MATERIALS

Measuring tape
12 small screw eyes
Picture hanging wire
Pliers

Screwdrivers
Wire cutters
Garden twine or other wrapping material

Lay the three cedar poles side by side. Measure and mark a screw eye location 24" from one end, and then 24" from the first mark. Lightly tap the point of the screw eyes into the marks using a hammer, and then screw them in using pliers or a screwdriver. Turn and repeat the process on the adjacent face of the pole.

Lean the poles together where they'll be placed in the garden, forming a loose teepee. (The screw eyes should be positioned on the inside two faces of all poles.) Tightly wrap a cord or twine around the neck of the teepee. You can also use any kind of durable, fairly weather-resistant material.

Wrap wire around one screw eye using the pliers. Stretch the wire to the same screw in an opposite leg, keeping the wire taut without pulling the legs any closer together (you can use temporary blocking if you're having trouble holding the legs in position while twisting the wire to secure it). Twist the wire around the second screw eye to secure it. Repeat with all the remaining screws. You should now be able to collapse the trellis as necessary to move it.

Teepee Trellis Alternatives

There is no lack of possibilities when it comes to the materials you can use for a teepee trellis pole. The two qualities you're looking for are durability in the face of excessive sun exposure (and all weather if you leave the trellis in position year-round), and a good strength-to-weight ratio. The stronger the material is, the heavier vegetables it can support, but if it's too light, it may need to be anchored in windy areas.

Here's a short list of common materials used in teepee trellises. Keep in mind, though, you can use anything that is non-toxic and will stay stiff under a load.

• **Bamboo.** Naturally strong, this "grass" is widely available as cut poles. Or, if you happen to have a stand of bamboo in your yard, you can cut your own bamboo poles for free. Bamboo is stiff enough to support lush vegetable growth, but it will degrade over time. In the meantime, it is one of the most attractive trellis poles you can use.

• **Branches/Found wood.** You'll have to hunt for just the right branches (hardwood preferred), but if you can locate branches that are 6 ft. long or longer, and wider than 1" in diameter, you'll probably have yourself a very rustic-looking, sturdy teepee trellis frame. Tie branches together with rough twine to carry through the look.

• **Reclaimed plumbing.** Long, skinny plumbing pipes are nearly indestructible poles for use in a teepee trellis. You don't want to reuse any plumbing that has carried waste or toxic materials, but otherwise, it will all work. It's strong, straight, and there are lots of ways to connect the poles for the teepee. The one big downside to a plumbing-pipe teepee trellis is the look. Most pipes are anything but handsome, but if looks are important to you, consider using copper pipes. Although the metal is attractive, you'll want to seal copper pipes because copper can be toxic to many plants.

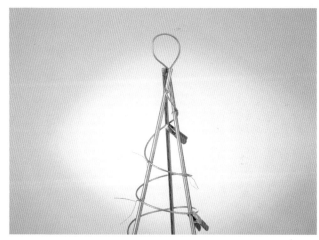

Pipes, like these copper plumbing tubes, make a lovely teepee trellis.

• **Dowels or tool handles.** These pieces of wood are well-suited for use in a teepee trellis. They come in standard sizes that make designing the trellis easy, and they are widely available and inexpensive. You can also choose from a range of diameters, depending on how firm you need the support to be.

Anchor Ideas

Stabilizing a teepee trellis is essential in a garden where kids, pets, or barnyard animals are regular visitors (or in any windy location—once the trellis is covered in vegetation, it becomes susceptible to wind). There are lots of ways to anchor a teepee trellis, but here are three that are very effective.

Buried Poles
The simplest way to secure the posts of the teepee is to bury the ends of the posts. This is an ideal solution where you are sure that you want the trellis to be a permanent fixture. Be aware that if the pole ends are not below the frost line in your area, the poles may heave up during the winter.

Potted Poles
This is the most interesting option. Pot up your climbing vegetables in large pots (usually, 2-gallon pots or larger). Before you fill the pots with soil around the plants, hold the poles in place and then backfill around them. It becomes a simple thing to grow the plant right up the pole as it matures. You can use just about any type of pot, giving you a lot of options as far as creating an interesting look at the base of your teepee.

Staked-Wire Teepee
Have an old orphan fence post or other buried pole in your garden? Put it to good use by running guy wires off it, to stakes in the ground. This is an exceptionally strong construction. The appearance depends on the central post, because the wires quickly become invisible underneath the vegetation. As a safety measure, tie strips of plastic to the wires for visibility, at least until the plants grow over the wires.

Jumbo Cold Frame

20

A cold frame of any size works on the same principle as a greenhouse, capturing sunlight and heat while protecting plants from cold winds and frost. But when your planting needs outgrow a basic backyard cold frame with a window-sash roof, it makes sense to look to the greenhouse for more comprehensive design inspiration. This jumbo version offers over 17 square feet of planting area and combines the convenience of a cold frame with the full sun exposure of a greenhouse. Plus, there's ample height under the cold frame's canopy for growing taller plants.

The canopy pivots on hinges and can be propped all the way up or partially opened to several different positions for ventilating the interior to control temperature. The hinges can be separated just like door hinges (in fact, they are door hinges), so you can remove the canopy for the off season, if desired. Clear polycarbonate roofing panels make the canopy lightweight yet durable, while admitting up to 90 percent of the sun's UV rays (depending on the panels you choose).

The base of the cold frame is a simple rectangle made with 2 × 6 lumber. You can pick it up and set it over an existing bed of plantings, or give it a permanent home, perhaps including a foundation of bricks or patio pavers to protect the wood from ground moisture. For additional frost protection and richer soil for your seedlings, dig down a foot or so inside the cold frame and work in a thick layer of mulch. Because all sides of the canopy have clear glazing, you don't have to worry about orienting the cold frame toward the sun; as virtually all of the interior space is equally exposed to light.

A cold frame can extend the growing season in your garden to almost—or truly—year round. Use an oversized cold frame like the one in this project and there may be no need to put up vegetables in the fall, because you'll have all the fresh produce you can handle.

Keeping Your Cold Frame Cool

Cold frames often can work too well, capturing and retaining so much heat that it becomes too hot for the plants, even during very cold weather. Adding an outdoor thermometer with a remote sensor (wired or wireless) lets you monitor the temp inside the cold frame without having to lift the canopy. Make sure the thermometer is rated for sub-freezing temperatures, since it will be exposed to the elements. Secure the sensor inside the frame as directed by the manufacturer. Mount the readout unit to the outside of the cold frame base. As an alternative, you can use a wireless system to send a readout to a thermometer inside the house. As a general guideline, the interior temperature of a cold frame should be no higher than 75°F for summer plants and 65°F or lower for spring and fall plants. But check the recommendations for your specific plantings.

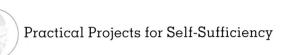

Building a Jumbo Cold Frame

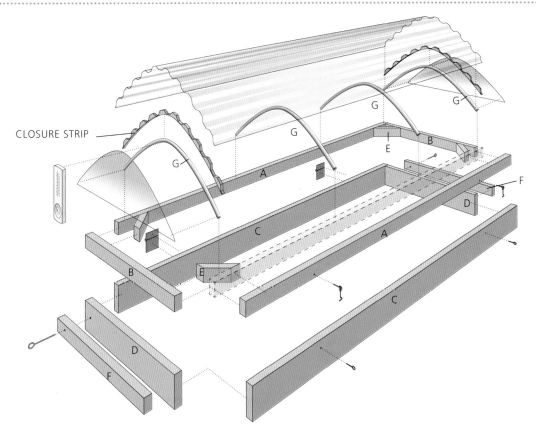

CLOSURE STRIP

CUTTING LIST

Key	No.	Part	Dimension	Material
A	2	Frame side	1½ x 2½ x 94"	2 x 3
B	2	Frame end	1½ x 2½ x 30"	2 x 3
C	2	Base side	1½ x 5½ x 94"	2 x 6
D	2	Base end	1½ x 5½ x 30"	2 x 6
E	4	Frame brace	1½ x 2½ x 8"	2 x 3
F	2	Prop stick	¾ x 1½ x 30"	1 x 2
G	4	Rib	½ x ½ x 37"	½ PVC tubing

TOOLS AND MATERIALS

Circular saw or miter saw
Cordless drill and bits
Hacksaw
Deck Screws 2," 2½," 3"
(5) ½" x 10-ft. thin wall PVC pipes (the flexible type
    used for lawn irrigation, not schedule 40 type)
(2) 25 x 96" corrugated polycarbonate roofing panels
30 x 24" clear acrylic panel

Roofing screws with EPDM washers
(2) 3½" exterior-grade butt hinges with screws
(2) ¼ x 4" eyebolts
3½ x ⁵⁄₁₆" stainless steel machine bolts
    (2 bolts with 8 washers and 2 nuts)
(2) Heavy-duty hook-and-eye latches
Outdoor thermometer with remote sensor

How to Build a Jumbo Cold Frame

Drill pilot holes and fasten the frame end pieces between the frame side pieces with 3" deck screws to create the rectangular frame. Do the same with the base pieces to create the base. Use two screws for each joint.

Stabilize the corners of the canopy frame with braces cut to 45° angles at both ends. Install the braces on-the-flat, so their top faces are flush with the tops of the canopy frame. Drill pilot holes and fasten through the braces and into the frame with one 2½" screw at each end. Then, drive one more screw through the outside of the frame and into each end of the brace. Check the frame for square as you work.

Assemble the canopy glazing framework using ½" PVC pipe. Cut all the ribs 37" long. You can cut these easily with a miter saw, hacksaw, or jigsaw.

Use 2" deck screws as receptors for the PVC pipes. Drive the screws in 1" from edge and ¾" from the ends, angling the screws at about 35 to 45° toward the center. Leave about ¾" of the screw exposed. Drive two additional screws in at 32¼" from each end.

Install the PVC ribs by putting one end over the 2" screw, then curving the PVC until the other end fits over the opposite screw. Take your time with this, and use a helper if you need. *Note:* Hopefully you've remembered to buy the flexible PVC, not the Schedule 40 type used for indoor plumbing.

(continued)

Hold up and mark a smooth piece of clear acrylic for the end panels. The clear acrylic should cover the 2 × 3 and follow the curving top of the PVC. Cut the clear acrylic with a plastic-cutting jigsaw blade.

Drill ¼" holes along the bottom of both panels about 5/8" up from the edge of the panel. Space the holes 2½" from ends, then every 16". Also mark and drill rib locations on the roof panels about 6" up from bottom, spacing the holes at 1⅝" and 33¼" from each end. Install the panels 1½" up from the bottom of the 2 × 3 with the roofing screws. The ends of the panels should extend 1" beyond the 2 × 3s.

Adjust the PVC ribs until the predrilled holes in the roof panels are centered on them, then predrill the PVC with a ⅛" bit. Fasten the panels to the two center ribs.

Lap the second sheet over the first, leaving roughly the same amount of panel hanging over the 2 × 3. Fasten the second sheet the same way as the first. Insert filler strips at each end under the polycarbonate, then drill through those into the PVC ribs. Now add additional screws about every ⅛". You can just predrill the holes with the ⅛" bit (the polycarbonate panels are soft enough that the screws will drive through them without cracking).

Set the clear acrylic end panels in place, butting them against the filler at the top. Mark screw locations. Place the panel on a piece of plywood and predrill with a ¼" diameter bit to avoid cracking the clear acrylic, which isn't as soft or flexible as the polycarbonate. Screw the panels in place with roofing screws, hand-tightening with a screwdriver to avoid cracking the clear acrylic. Don't overtighten.

Mount the canopy to the cold frame base with two exterior hinges. The canopy frame should fit flush over the base on all sides. Screw in two hook-and-eye latches in front.

Attach a prop stick to each side with a stainless steel bolt and nut. Insert three washers (or more) between the prop stick and the 2 × 6 base so the prop stick clears the clear acrylic side panel. Drill a few additional ⁵⁄₁₆" holes in the stick and the frame for the eyebolts, so that you can prop the canopy open at different heights. Now, prepare the ground and place the cold frame in the desired location. Anchor the base to the ground using 16" treated stakes or heavy-duty metal anges driven into the ground and secured to the frame.

Raised Bed With Removable Trellis

It's hard to beat PVC plumbing pipe for adding a trellis to a simple raised bed. It's inexpensive and rot-proof and goes together like pieces of a toy construction set. It's also durable, lightweight, and can stand up to just about anything the elements can throw at it.

This all-purpose trellis is made almost entirely with PVC parts and is designed to be custom-fit to your raised bed. For a bed with 2× lumber sides, you can secure the trellis uprights to the outside of the bed with metal pipe straps. If the sides of the bed are built with timbers, the trellis simply drops into holes drilled into the tops of the timbers. Of course, you can get much more creative with the configuration if you want to bump up your yield. Add another, identical trellis to the opposite end of a longer raised bed. Or add three—at either end and in the middle—of a really long bed. Making the most of vertical space with a trellis is a great way to grow a lot more vegetables in the same footprint. This can be key if you're looking to put up a lot of vegetables for over the winter.

The trellis as shown is made with 1½-inch PVC pipe and fittings. The parts are friction fit only, so they are not glued together and can easily be disassembled for off-season storage. PVC pipe and fittings are manufactured for a very tight fit; if you push the pipe all the way into the fittings, the joints won't come apart unless you want them to. Separate the joints by twisting the pipe or fitting while pulling straight out. Due to the tight fit, it doesn't help to try to wiggle it loose.

PVC pipe and fittings come in one color: stark white. You may want to paint your trellis to blend in with your garden setting, but this isn't necessary. Once it becomes covered with lush plant growth, the appearance of the pipe will be much less noticeable. Exposure to sunlight somewhat dulls PVC over time, but this doesn't significantly affect its strength.

Raised Box Trellis Options

The basic design of this bed-and-trellis combination lends itself to customization. If, for instance, you want a sturdier trellis to support much heavier plants or stand up to high winds, you can swap the PVC pipes and fittings for metal plumbing pipes and fittings. Better yet, if you want to add a rustic appeal to your unit, you can use copper pipes—just seal the copper so that it doesn't contaminate your plants. The box itself can easily be fabricated from found lumber, or lumber reclaimed from construction sites (just ask the site supervisor or foreman before you go dumpster diving). The only requirement is that the wood you reuse not be treated in any way. Otherwise, free is the best price for a self-sufficient project!

A raised bed box made from 2 x 6 lumber is used as the base for a sturdy built-in trellis made of PVC tubing. It's the ideal support for heavy climbing plants like beans or cucumbers.

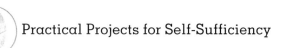
Building a Raised Bed With Removable Trellis

CUTTING LIST

Key	No.	Part	Dimension	Material
A	2	Side	1½ x 5½ x 72"	2 x 6 cedar
B	2	End	1½ x 5½ x 36"	2 x 6 cedar
C	2	Upper vertical	1½ x 60"	PVC pipe
D	2	Lower vertical	1½ x 12"	PVC pipe
E	2	Crosspiece	1½ x 34"	PVC pipe

TOOLS AND MATERIALS

(2) 1½" x 10 ft. PVC pipe
(2) 1½" PVC 90° elbows
(2) 1½" PVC T-fittings
Heavy jute or hemp twine
Pipe straps for 1½" PVC (4 screw type)
Metal inside corners
Deck Screws 1¼," 2½"
Tape measure
Cordless drill and bits
Hacksaw or miter saw
Sandpaper
Scissors or utility knife

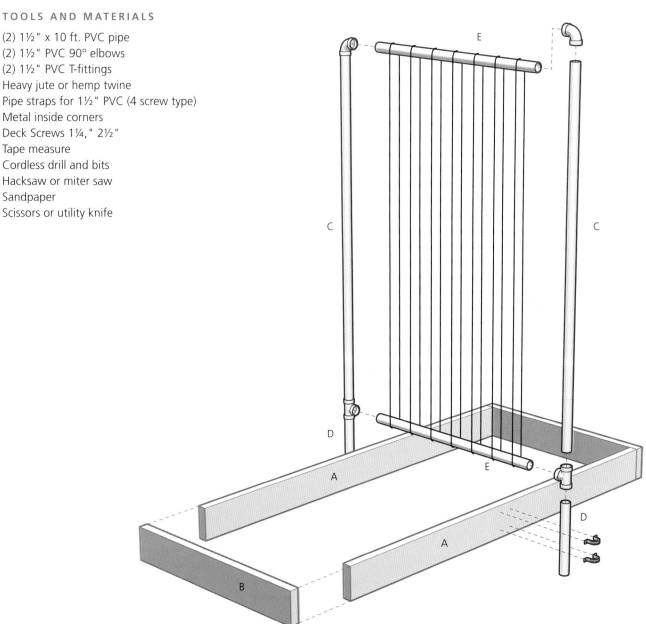

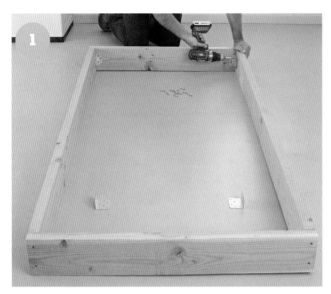

Start by assembling the raised-bed box, reinforcing the joints with metal inside corners. Add a center divider to keep the sides from spreading apart if you decide to make this project longer than 6'. Even if it is shorter, the divider is still a good precaution to help prevent warping.

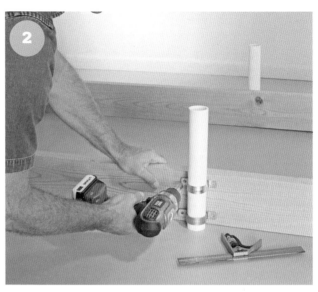

Cut 12"-long pieces of 1½" PVC tubing. Attach them to the outsides of the planter box, near the middle. Use emery paper or sandpaper to remove the burrs and smooth the cut ends of pipe. Draw a perpendicular line where the pipe will go, using a square. Strap the pieces to the outsides with two pipe straps each. Fasten one strap with two screws, but leave the other strap loose until you put the upper vertical PVC on and can check it for plumb.

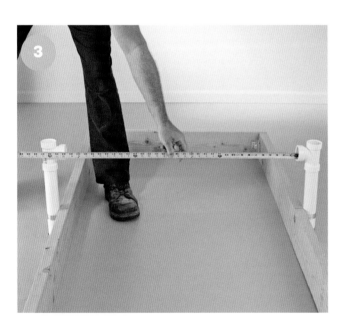

Add a T-fitting to the top end of each pipe. Measure between the hubs of the T-fittings to the insides of the sockets. Cut a piece of 1½" PVC pipe to this length and sand the cut edges smooth; this is the bottom cross piece. Remove both Ts, fit the piece into the middle hubs of the Ts so the ends of the pipe bottom out in the fittings. Then replace the Ts.

Add the uprights and attach the top crosspiece with elbows. Ensure the pipes are plumb, then secure the bottom straps. Move the planter into your yard or garden, line it with a thick layer of old newspaper or landscape fabric, and fill it with planting medium. Tie jute or hemp twine between the crosspieces so that climbing plants have something to grab onto. When winter comes, you can disassemble the PVC and store it away until spring.

Pallet Planter

Pallets are so abundant in this country that they're often just left by the curb for people to take as firewood. Despite this lack of perceived value, they can actually be quite useful to the thrift-minded self-sufficient homeowner. They can be perfect for a wide variety of recycled projects like compost bins, furniture, fuel and, yes, planters.

Because pallets have to support thousands of pounds, they're generally made from tough hardwoods without big knots. When the wood is cleaned up and sanded, it can look surprisingly attractive. Pallet wood may not last as long outdoors as cedar or treated wood (unless you find a pallet made from white oak), but since it's free you can just replace it when it rots. In the meantime, it looks great.

There are many different ways to turn a pallet into a planter, but don't count on just pulling out all the nails and reusing all the pieces. It can be done, but hardwood grips nails a lot tighter than the softwoods used for construction lumber, and the wood slats often crack before the nail pulls out. (It's wise to always grab a few extra pallets for any project, precisely for this reason.) If you have to remove a few pieces, lever carefully under the wood slats, and use a reciprocating saw outfitted with a metal-cutting blade to cut nails that are hard to pull. However, the easiest way to use pallets is as is—as we've done in this project. We designed this one to be vertical, but you can also lay it flat and stack a few underneath so that the plants are at a comfortable height, or combine several in a stairstep design.

Look for pallets in industrial and commercial areas. If you're lucky, you'll see a big pile with a "Free" sign on them, but you can also find them poking out of dumpsters or just piled up in a parking lot. If in doubt, always ask if you can take them. Most will be dirty and have a cracked or missing slat, but if you grab an extra you can use it for parts.

TIP

Pallet Shopping

There is actually a good deal of information stamped on every pallet. Obviously, you should avoid those that look heavily oil-stained, or smell of chemicals. But beyond that, you can find the label on the pallet and use it to tell you something about the wood itself. The stamp will usually show the logo of the company who produced it. It will also list what country it was made in, and—most importantly—it will list a code that usually starts with "DB" (de-backed) and includes two letters that indicate how the wood was treated. "HT" means the wood was heat treated and will be fine for use in contact with soil. "MB" means the wood was treated with the pesticide methyl bromide, and should probably not be used for food crops.

Upcycling is a key part of any self-sufficient household, and pallets are some of the handiest candidates for the treatment. For this vertical planter project, the pallet is left intact and converted for use in a smaller area such as a patio, deck, or balcony. All part of turning every corner of the yard into a productive part of the whole.

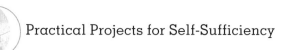
Making a Pallet Planter

After brushing off the dirt and renailing any loose boards, use some 80-grit sandpaper to clean up the areas that will be visible. Also round over rough, splintery edges. Paint or finish the outside of the pallet, if desired, but don't finish the inside if you're planting edibles.

Making the Planter

The process used to turn this pallet into a planter is a simple one and can be done by anyone with even very basic DIY skills. Decide which end of the pallet will be up, then cover openings at the back to keep dirt from falling out through the openings.

Gaps on the sides will be covered with a strip of metal flashing, an extra slat or a piece of wood cut to size. The back is covered with rubber pond liner or a double layer of black 6-mil poly (but make sure none of it is exposed to the sun, or it will decay).

Finally, nail a doubled-over strip of aluminum screen mesh across the bottom of the pallet to keep the dirt in, and then fill with top soil. Tamp it down with a long stick to make sure the pallet fills up. Dirt will fall out the front at first, but will settle in at an angle behind each opening.

You can simply lean the planter against a wall in a sunny area if you prefer. However, you can also mount the planter on a southern or eastern-facing side of a garage, house, or outbuilding. If you prefer to put the planter out in the garden or in a sunny spot in the yard, you can screw stakes to each side or front and back, and then secure it in the ground so that it doesn't fall over when bumped or on a windy day.

If space is tight, you can even wire it to a balcony or deck railing. Just be sure the railing is solid because when you water the plants and soil in the planter, it can become fairly heavy.

Pallet Planter Options

You can make individual planters using the same method described here, but by cutting the pallet into sections. You can also decorate the pallet to better suit the style of the yard. As long as you don't get any paint inside, you can paint the outside in different colors or even stain the wood if you prefer.

Planting Your Pallet Planter

As you examine your completed pallet planter, one question immediately comes to mind: Won't all the dirt fall out the front? Well, if you did not plant any plants in it the answer is yes, it will. However, you are relying on the plant roots and the 2 x 2 shelves you installed to hold things together. To add plants, lay the planter flat on its back and plan to keep it that way for a couple of weeks. Pack the gaps full of potting soil (potting soil is pre-fertilized, unlike topsoil) and then pack in as many seedlings as you can fit. Water the plants for a couple of weeks so the roots can establish. Then, tip the planter up against the wall in position. A little soil may trickle out initially, but you should find that everything holds together nicely.

Best Pallet Plants

Not every vegetable or fruit will be at home in a pallet planter, but it can serve as the ideal location for several garden favorites.

Strawberries. Just as in a strawberry pot, these plants are at home with the shallow soil in the planter "pockets". The plants are easy to work with and, once settled in the planter, will produce a crop for several years.

Leaf lettuces. The plants will spread out in the pockets and, if kept watered and reasonably cool (you may need to shade the planter during the hottest part of the day), they will thrive in the planter.

Herbs. A pallet planter is idea for an herb garden. Because you only need a small amount of each herb, the planter can support an entire kitchen herb garden. It can also be set against a wall right outside a kitchen door, making the herbs incredibly convenient for harvesting.

TOOLS AND MATERIALS

Cedar 2 x 2s, cut to fit
Cordless drill and bits
Screwdriver or pry bar
2" deck screws
Staple gun and staples
Pond liner or 6-mil poly
Scrap wood
Aluminum screen mesh

Cut the 2 × 2 shelves to the length for the cavities in your pallet and fit them in on the lower edge of each slat. Predrill and toenail at each end to hold them in place, then drive an additional screw into the cedar from the front. Pallet wood is hard, so drill pilot holes for all screws. *Note:* Most pallets have a good face and a bad face. Be sure that you are creating your planter so the face with the nicer decking will point away from the wall you are installing it against.

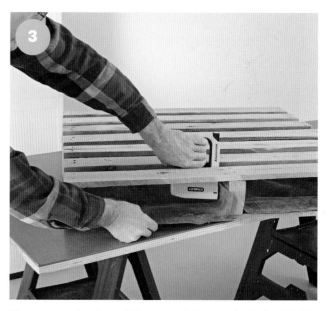

Stiffen the pallet and provide a surface for attaching the liner. Fill the gaps on the back side with wood scraps of roughly the same thickness as the back boards.

Measure and cut pond liner or poly sheeting for the back. Fold the liner onto the sides and staple it in place on the sides and back. You can use heavy black poly sheeting to make the liner, but for a more durable material use roll rubber. Staple aluminum screen mesh across the bottom of the pallet.

Raising Animals

A big part of self-sufficiency is producing your own food. But as delicious and nutritious as fruits and vegetables may be, protein is an important part of every diet. That's where food animals come in, especially chickens. Chickens provide an ongoing harvest of eggs and can supply valuable meat as well.

Beyond food, some living additions to your self-sufficient homestead provide support in different ways. Goats give you milk, which can be processed into cheese. Bees provide a valuable service in pollinating garden plants and supply delicious honey in the bargain—making them some of the most beneficial living things you can raise on your property. They also require very little care and upkeep, making them even more desirable for any homestead looking to become self-sufficient with a minimum of free time.

The projects in this section are all about taking the best care possible of the animals that call your home, well, home. These structures are specifically designed and suited to a given creature, but they have also been designed to look good. These are simple structures—you won't need homebuilding experience to put up the chicken coop we outline in the pages that follow, nor will you need to be a master woodworker to assemble your own honey-making beehive.

With a little bit of work and a modicum of tools and materials, you can make homes within your homestead for living things that will help you live more self-sufficiently.

Chicken Coop

One of the simplest and most classic designs for a chicken coop is a box with a sloping, shed-style roof. This traditional form is straightforward and makes for an inherently sturdy structure with ample interior space to let chickens enjoy their favorite indoor activities; namely, roosting (sleeping) and laying eggs. With a compact footprint that makes it a good choice for city chickens and their country cousins alike, this coop has a couple of modern twists.

The walls, floor and roof are panelized with homemade SIPs (structural insulated panels). SIPs are plywood (or other sheet material) sandwiched over rigid foam insulation board, resulting in a structurally sound building unit that doesn't need an internal framework of studs, joists, or rafters. Instead, a single band of lumber along the edges protects and hides the insulation and provides a fastening surface for the panel assembly. Best of all, the panels are insulated, and while you might not think a chicken coop needs to be energy-efficient, insulation helps keep a coop cooler in hot weather and warmer when it's cold.

Other special features of this coop include:
- Clerestory windows in front
- Tapered window and ventilation openings along each side
- Front door that swings down and doubles as a ramp for the chickens
- Rear door that swings up and locks open for access to the coop interior for harvesting eggs and cleaning
- Paint-on, elastomeric roof covering

All of the plywood parts for this chicken coop can be cut from six 4 x 8 sheets of ½" plywood if you follow the following plan (note that the roof panels are too large to come from one sheet and are made using two pieces of plywood).

Sheet 1:
A Front wall (outer)
B Front wall (inner)
O Rear door (inner)
P Rear wall filler

Sheet 2:
D (1) Side wall (outer)
E (1) Side wall (inner)
N Rear door (outer)

Sheet 3:
D (1) Side wall (outer)
E (1) Side wall (inner)
G Roof panels (partial)

Sheet 4:
G Roof panel (partial)
K Rear wall (outer)

Sheet 5:
G Roof panel (partial)
L Rear wall (inner)

Sheet 6:
I (2) Floor panels
FF Front door

This insulated chicken coop is a cozy home for two to four chickens, and it's also handy for the chicken keeper because it's easy to clean. Its classic red barn styling make it a good-looking yard addition to boot.

Building a Chicken Coop

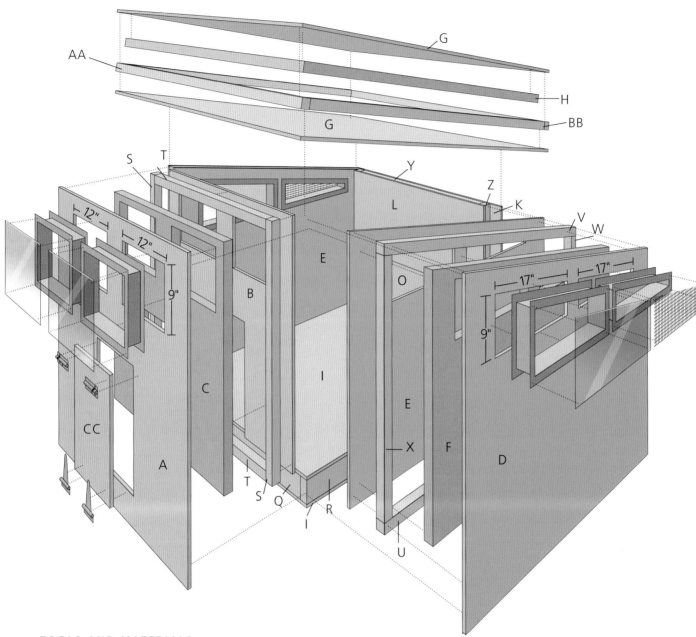

TOOLS AND MATERIALS

Circular saw
Jigsaw
Keyhole saw
Miter saw (optional)
Cordless drill and bits
Utility knife or handsaw
2½" metal track
Dust mask
Aviation snips
Staple gun
Caulking gun

Deck screws, 1⅝"
Panhead screws, 1"
4 x 8 sheets 1½" XPS or EPS rigid
   foam insulation board
⅛"-thick acrylic sheeting (1 piece
   17 x 20" min.; one piece 10 x 30" min.)
Clear silicone caulk
½ x ½" galvanized hardware cloth
   (12 x 17" min.)
Heavy-duty staples
Construction adhesive

(5) Heavy-duty exterior strap hinges
   with screws
(4) Exterior barrel-bolt latches
(2) Heavy-duty exterior
   hook-and-eye latches
(4) Concrete blocks (as desired)
Drip-edge molding
Elastomeric roof coating
Handle

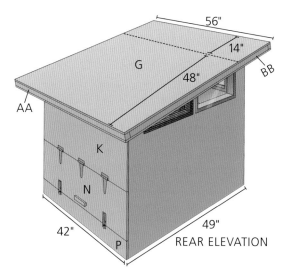

REAR ELEVATION

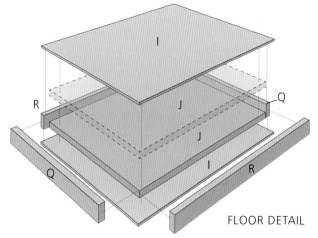

FLOOR DETAIL

CUTTING LIST

Key	No.	Part	Dimension	Material
A	1	Front wall (outer)	½ x 42 x 42"	Ext. grade plywood
B	1	Front wall (inner)	½ x 37 x 37"	Ext. grade plywood
C	1	Front wall insulation	1½ x 34 x 34"	Foam insulation
D	2	Side wall (outer)	½ x 42 x 42"	Ext. grade plywood
E	2	Side wall (inner)	½ x 42 x 37½"	Ext. grade plywood
F	2	Side wall insulation	1½ x 39 x 34½"	Foam insulation
G	2	Roof panel	½ x 56 x 62"	Ext. grade plywood
H	1	Roof insulation	1½ x 53 x 59"	Foam insulation
I	2	Floor panel	½ x 36 x 37"	Ext. grade plywood
J	2	Floor insulation	1½ x 33 x 34"	Foam insulation
K	1	Rear wall (outer)	½ x 42 x 21"	Ext. grade plywood
L	1	Rear wall (inner)	½ x 37 x 21"	Ext. grade plywood
M	1	Rear wall insulation (not visible)	1½ x 34 x 18"	Foam insulation
N	1	Rear door (outer)	½ x 12 x 42"	Ext. grade plywood
O	1	Rear door (inner)	½ x 11½ x 36 3/4"	Ext. grade plywood
P	1	Rear wall filler	½ x 4½ x 42"	Ext. grade plywood
Q	2	Floor frame end	1½ x 3½ x 33"	2 x 4
R	2	Floor frame side	1½ x 3½ x 37"	2 x 4
S	2	Front frame side	1½ x 1½ x 37"	2 x 2
T	2	Front frame end	1½ x 1½ x 34"	2 x 2
U	2	Side frame bottom	1½ x 1½ x 48"	2 x 2
V	2	Side frame top	1½ x 1½ x 48⅞"	2 x 2
W	2	Side frame back	1½ x 1½ x 30"	2 x 2
X	2	Side frame front	1½ x 1½ x 39"	2 x 2
Y	2	Rear wall frame end	1½ x 1½ x 39"	2 x 2
Z	2	Rear wall frame side	1½ x 1½ x 16½"	2 x 2
AA	2	Roof frame end	1½ x 1½ x 56"	2 x 2
BB	2	Roof frame side	1½ x 1½ x 59"	2 x 2
CC	1	Front door	½ x 12 x 18"	Ext. grade plywood

*Windows are custom fabricated from metal stud track, clear acrylic and hardware cloth

Cut the plywood parts (see page 142). Use a circular saw and guide for straight cuts. Lay out the cutouts for the windows, ventilation openings, and front door according to the measurements on page 142. Make the cutouts by plunge-cutting with a jigsaw (or drilling a starter hole and then completing the cuts).

Add the perimeter frame pieces for each panel assembly. The floor frame is made with 2 × 4s; all other panels are constructed with 2 × 2s. The vertical frame pieces on the side walls are angled at 10° on their top ends. A miter saw is ideal for cutting the framing, but a circular saw works just fine. Install the framing pieces to the exterior plywood panels with 1½" deck screws driven through the outside faces of the plywood and into the framing.

Measure each area inside the panel framing and cut 1½"-thick insulation board to fit. You can use XPS or EPS insulation (XPS is more expensive but offers a higher R-value for the same thickness). Wear a good dust mask or respirator during cutting. Each panel gets one layer of insulation, except for the floor, which gets two layers (3" total). Extend the cutouts in the plywood through the insulation board after the panels are assembled.

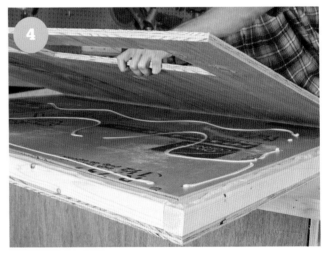

Line the window openings with 2½" metal track (for metal stud walls). You'll need to bend the track to fit, which requires that you make a relief cut in the flange at each corner, using aviation snips. Once you have framed all windows, cut the acrylic sheeting to size so each window extends beyond all edges of its opening. Apply a thin bead of silicone caulk around each opening (on the inner wall), and set the glazing into the caulk. Let the caulk set up and then drive a 1" panhead screw near each corner, drilling guide holes in the acrylic first. Staple ½" hardware cloth over the ventilation opening at the rear end of each side wall.

Assemble the panels by gluing the insulation to the inside faces of the plywood with construction adhesive (make sure the adhesive is compatible with the insulation material). Screw the plywood panels to the framing with 1⅝" deck screws. Seal any seam between the plywood pieces (in the roof panels) with silicone caulk before fastening. Make cutouts in the insulation board using a keyhole saw.

Set a sidewall onto the floor panel, with the plywood edge lapping over the edge of the bottom panel. Working with a helper, set the front panel next to the side panel and fasten them together at the corner. Screw the side walls through the plywood into the floor frame with 1⅝" deck screws. Install the upper, fixed portion of the rear panel so that the exterior plywood is flush with the tops of the side walls. Finally, install the roof, screwing up through the framing of the side panels and into the interior roof plywood (from inside the coop).

Assemble the rear door, which is simply two pieces of plywood laminated together—no insulation. Hang the rear door using three evenly spaced hinges mounted along the top edge of the door panel. Check that it opens and closes freely and can swing up flush against the fixed rear panel above. Install two hook-and-eye latches on the door and fixed panel. Add a gate latch at each side of the door. (It's important that all door closures are secure to protect the chickens.) Cover the edge of the floor panel below the rear door, using the precut filler strip of plywood.

Add trim and additional hardware as desired. For the roof, drip-edge molding was installed to conceal the edge grain of the plywood. Then several coats of elastomeric roof covering were spread on with a paintbrush. Paint or finish the exterior as desired. Set the coop onto four concrete blocks or bricks—it will be heavy so get some helpers. Hang the front door using two hinges mounted to the bottom of the door and the floor panel below. Test the door's operation, then install a barrel bolt on each side of the door to keep it securely shut against predators.

Brooder Box

Expectant parents of both human and chicken babies get the same advice: Have the nursery ready before you bring home the little one(s). You'll enjoy those precious first weeks a lot more if you're not running around like a . . . well, never mind. For chickens, a nursery is a brooder box, and it's used to provide the same essentials human newborns need: security, warmth, and nourishment. The nice thing about a chicken nursery is that you don't have worry about wall color or getting an ultrasound if you absolutely refuse to go gender-neutral (you're probably expecting all girls anyway).

A brooder box can be literally that simple—just a cardboard box, or a plastic bin, an old fish tank, even a kiddie pool. Backyard farmers often use whatever they have on hand. But a nice, sturdy wood box with a few convenience and safety features will make raising your chicks a better experience, for this brood and many more down the road. This brooder box is made with a single sheet of ¾ inches plywood and measures 36 × 36 × 17⅜-inches, enough room for housing 8 to 10 chicks up to six weeks old. Both the lid and the floor are covered with hardware cloth (wire mesh), making the box secure, well-ventilated, and easy to clean.

Heat is provided by a simple clamp-on reflector light, which can be set directly atop the lid's wire mesh or clamped to the light pole at various heights for temperature control. The box lid is hinged in the back and locks in the front with a locking hasp latch. Special removable hinges make it easy to slide off the lid to get it out of the way for a thorough cleaning of the box.

A brooder box like this is a nursery to your newborn chicks, so it's essential that it be comfortable, warm, safe and nurturing to your future chickens.

TIP

On Lights and Litter

You can use a range of materials for the litter, or bedding, in your brooder box, including pine shavings (not cedar or redwood), shredded paper, chopped straw, and sand, but the best thing for the first week or so is a few layers of paper towels. These create a flat but soft surface that's easy for new chicks to walk on, and the layer is absorbent and easy to replace for cleanup. After the chicks are moving around well and eating heartily, you can switch to other bedding material. Whatever bedding you're using, you can start with a foundation of a newspaper over the mesh bottom of the box to help contain the bedding and provide a flat foundation. Don't use newspaper by itself because it's too slippery for new chicks learning to walk.

Lighting—that is, heating—the brooder box properly often requires some fine-tuning to get the temperature just right, as well as periodic adjustments as the chicks mature. With a simple clamp-on light setup shown here, you can easily adjust the heat by raising or lowering the light. Watch the chicks' behavior to determine the right temperature: If they seem to be avoiding the circle of light underneath the fixture, it may be too hot. If they huddle together directly under the light, the chicks are too cold. And if they move easily around the space like socialites at a charity gala, they're probably just right. The standard heat source for brooding boxes is a 250-watt infrared heat lamp/bulb. Make sure the fixture is rated for 250 watts to prevent a fire hazard. Many chicken raisers feel that chickens do best with a red light, rather than the harsh white of standard bulbs. You can buy heat lamp/bulbs and fixtures at farm supply stores and some home centers.

Building a Brooder Box

CUTTING LIST

Key	No.	Part	Dimension	Material
A	1	Top	¾ x 36 x 36"	¾" Plywood
B	2	End	¾ x 36 x 15⅞"	¾" Plywood
C	2	Side	¾ x 34½ x 15⅞"	¾" Plywood
D	2	Handle	1½ x 3½ x 6"	2 x 4
E	4	Base	¾ x 1½"	1 x 2
F	1	Light mount	1½ x 3½ x 6"	2 x 4

TOOLS AND MATERIALS

Circular saw
Drill
Jigsaw
Wire cutters
Staple gun
Wood glue

Deck Screws 1¼," 2"
½" x ½" galvanized hardware
　cloth (36 x 70" min.)
Heavy-duty ½" staples
½"-diameter x 36"-long
　hardwood dowel

(2) Separable lid hinges with screws
Locking hasp latch with screws
Clamp-on light fixture
Zip ties (optional)

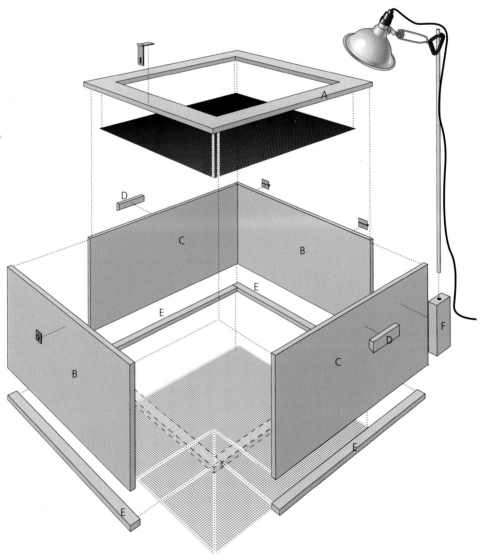

Make the lid cutout by marking four lines 4" from the outside edges of the lid piece. Carefully lower your circular saw onto one end of the line and cut to the other end. Finish the cuts at the corners with a jigsaw. *Tip:* Roughly lay out the parts on the plywood sheet before marking and cutting the pieces one at a time.

Create the two handles, beveling one long edge at 15°. Cut the strip in half to end up with two 6"-long handles. Install the handles with glue and 1⅝" deck screws so the top edges of the handles are about 2" below the top of the box sides. The long beveled edges face down and toward the box side, creating an easy-to-grab lip for each handle. *Inset:* Construct the light pole mount by drilling a ½" centered hole in the end of a scrap 2 × 4. Ream the hole until the dowel fits easily and can be slipped in and out to facilitate box cleanings.

Assemble the box frame using glue and 2" deck screws. Fit the front and back pieces over the ends of the sides, drill pilot holes, then apply glue and fasten each joint with five evenly spaced screws. Use a framing square to make sure the corners are square as you work. Sand all exposed edges of the box and lid.

Use wire cutters to cut the box bottom and lid cover from ½" hardware cloth. Cut the bottom to 35¾ × 35¾"; cut the lid cover 34 × 34". Screw 1 × 2 cleats to the bottom edges of the plywood box frame, then staple on the bottom cloth with heavy-duty ½" staples. Keep the edges of the mesh ⅛" from the outside edges of the box on all sides. Staple the lid cover to the underside of the lid frame, keeping the mesh 1" from all outside edges. Use plenty of staples on the cover—and staple close to the edges of the cutout—to prevent predators from pushing down the mesh.

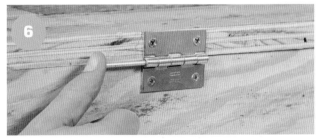

Install the box lid using two separable hinges (also called removable or lift-away hinges). Depending on the hinge design, you may want to recess the hinge plates on the box by cutting shallow mortises, using a wood chisel. Add a locking hasp latch to the front side so the lid can lock securely to the box front. Clamp the light fixture to the dowel and plug it in to test the setup.

Beehive

A traditional beehive is an ideal addition to the self-sufficient homestead. Create a welcoming home for a colony of bees and you ensure pollination for the plants in your garden, add to the health of your local ecosystem, and produce a bumper crop of beekeeper's gold—better known as sweet, delicious honey.

The 10-frame hive design shown here is familiar to anyone who has passed an active orchard or seen beekeepers in action. It is formally known as a Langstroth Hive, and is the standard for beehives. It features a basic construction meant to accommodate removable frames into which bees build honeycombs. Depending on where the frame is in the hive, the bees will use the honeycomb for brooding—to raise new bees—or to hold honey. The discovery that led the Reverend Lorenzo Lorraine Langstroth to develop this design was that a specific spacing—$\frac{5}{32}$-inches to be exact—was ideal to allow bees to move around in the hive. The space is too small for bees to fill in with honeycomb, and too large for them to try to close it up with the wax-like material propolis. That meant that the frames were left free to be removed. The beekeeper could easily take out a diseased section or remove frames to harvest honey. The design has been used around the world ever since.

Although it may look like a complex project, a beehive is fairly simple in construction. Building a beehive begins at the bottom, with what is know as the "bottom board." There are three types of bottom boards: solid; screened, and slatted. A screened bottom board is used where varroa mites are active and where the bees will pick them up. The screen allows for the mites to fall down and through the screen, so that they can't get back to the bees. The slatted bottom rack is a complex construction that further protects the hive by improving air circulation, adds additional cluster space for the bees, and prevents swarming. Any bottom board is built slightly longer than the hive bodies, to leave room for bees to enter and leave. This project describes how to build a basic solid bottom board. Once you've built that, it's easy to find plans and construct a screened bottom board or slatted bottom rack, should you think either of those necessary for your hive. Some beekeepers use a combination, especially in bigger and busier hives.

A Simple, Easy-to-Build Hive Stand

You'll need to use some type of stand to get your hive up off the ground and away from potential predators. The stand should also maintain a bit of air circulation around the hive. This basic unit shown here can be made in minutes with a few pieces of lumber and some screws. Mark and drill pilot holes through the brace faces down into the base 4 x 4s. Screw the braces to the base using 4" deck screws and you're finished! You can add 4 x 4 legs to the base if you prefer to the keep the hive even higher.

A traditional beehive such as this can serve as the perfect home for your own busy colony … and a gathering place for delicious honey.

Sitting atop the bottom board are two or more body sections. There are actually two types of these: the deeper "hive bodies" that house the brood, or young bees (in all stages), and the upper honey "super", which contains the honeycombs filled with honey. Both house rows of suspended frames.

The boxes are simple in construction but can be built in a number of different ways. We've chosen the simplest style of construction—butt joints—but if you have woodworking experience and want to take your hive construction to the next level, you can use rabbeted or dovetailed joints. Both will be stronger than butt joints. The number of hive bodies and supers you include depends on a couple of factors. A regular or small population of bees will normally require only one hive body. If you add bees, you'll need another. Supers range

in depths. If you've chosen thin supers to make the honey frames easier to handle, or if you have enough bees to require two bodies, you'll want more than one super. In any case, we've included one hive body and one super in this project for purposes of clarity in illustrating the details.

No matter how many bodies or supers you include, they'll need to be capped by a top. Most hives include an inner cover with a hole that permits movement in and out of the cover, and an outer cover that fits completely over the top structure to seal the hive and protect it from predators and the elements. You can also choose a screened inner cover that allows for better air circulation and enables you to inspect your hive without unduly disturbing the bees or having to remove the inner cover.

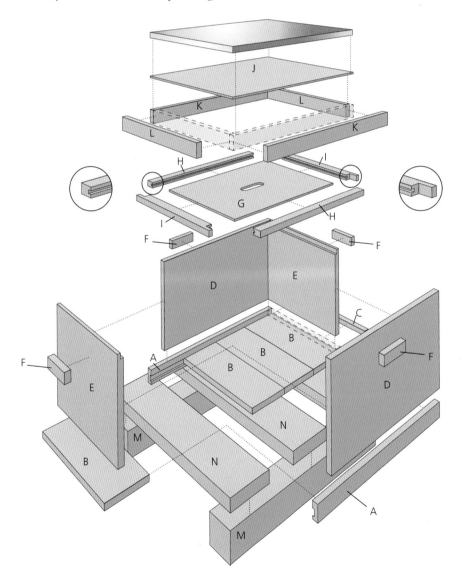

Building a Bee Hive

Lastly, we've included instructions for a very basic hive stand. Hives are not placed on the ground for a variety of reasons, and a stand like the one shown here ensures that the hive is portable, should it need to be moved. You can choose a more fixed design by attaching legs to the bottom of the bottom board, or simply place your hive on a table or sawhorses.

You can make your own beehive frames from scratch, but given the intricate and repetitive woodworking involved, the vast majority of hive owners buy pre-made frame kits for the standard frame, called "Dadant frames" (available online or from stores that stock beehive equipment). The kits include all the components necessary to build the frames, along with detailed instructions.

CUTTING LIST
Bottom Board

Key	No.	Part	Dimension	Material
A	2	Side	1⅞ x ¾ x 22 "	1 x 3
B	4	Bottom	¾ x 5½ x 15¼ "	1 x 6
C	1	Filler strip	¾ x ¾ x 14¾ "	1 x 1

Hive Body

Key	No.	Part	Dimension	Material
D	2	Side	¾ x 11¼ x 19⅞ "	1 x 12
E	2	End	¾ x 11¼ x 14¾ "	1 x 12
F	4	Handle	¾ x 1½ x 4 "	1 x 2

Inner Cover

Key	No.	Part	Dimension	Material
G	1	Center board	¼ x 14¼ x 17⅞ "	1/4 " plywood
H	2	Side trim	¾ x 1¼ x 18⅞ "	1 x 2
I	2	End trim	¾ x 1¼ x 16¼ "	1 x 2

Outer Cover

Key	No.	Part	Dimension	Material
J	1	Top	¼ x 21⅞ x 18¼ "	¼ " plywood
K	2	Side	¾ x 1¾ x 21⅞ "	1 x 3
L	2	End	¾ x 1¾ x 16 ¾ "	1 x 3

Hive Stand

Key	No.	Part	Dimension	Material
M	2	Base	3½ x 3½ x 24 "	4 x 4
N	3	Brace	1¾ x 5½ x 24 "	2 x 6

TOOLS AND MATERIALS

Cordless drill and bits
Miter saw
Tablesaw and dado blade
Jigsaw
23⅜ x 20" aluminum flashing
   or a premade hive top
1¼ " deck screws
Deck screws 2," 4"
¾ " sheet metal screws or roofing nails
Waterproof wood glue
Sandpaper
Bar or pipe clamps
Tin snips
Rubber mallet

On a table saw, cut the dado in each side piece using a dado blade. (You can also use a router with a ¾" straight bit.) Start with a 1 x 6 to make it easier and safer to cut the dados, then rip the board to 1⅞" wide. Set the fence ¾" from the blade, with the blade height ¼". For safety, clamp a temporary top of scrap plywood to the table and raise the dado blade through it. Make the dado cut slightly wider than ¾". It's a good idea to test cut a scrap piece and check it for fit with the bottom boards. Then rip the dadoed sides to 1⅞" wide.

Optional: A tongue-and-groove construction will be stronger than the butt joints used in this project, but it is also a lot more work to cut all pieces with the tongues and grooves. A compromise that improves the strength of the bottom board but takes less time is lap-joint construction. Set a table saw blade height to ⅜" and set the fence to ⅜" measured to the outside of the blade. Cut top and bottom half laps on each side of the middle boards, and one top and one bottom lap on either end board.

Dry fit the pieces to ensure there are no gaps. Apply the glue along the inside edges of the boards and in the dado of the side pieces. Assemble the pieces and wipe away any glue squeeze out. Clamp the entire assembly using bar or pipe clamps, until the glue dries.

Use a square or straightedge to mark the center of the dado along the outside face of the side pieces. Drill pilot holes through the outside faces of the side pieces into the edges of the bottom boards. Drill two holes per side for each outside board and one hole for the inside boards, then drive screws through the side pieces into the bottom boards. Do the same with the filler strip at one end of the construction.

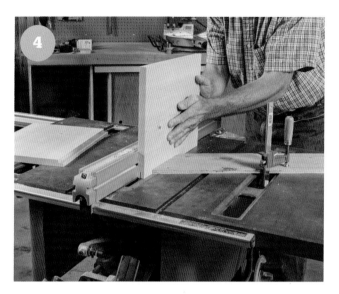

Set up the table saw to cut rabbets along the top edge of both end pieces. Set the fence to ⅜" measured to the outside of the blade, and the blade height to ⅝". Push the end piece through on end. (A featherboard, shown here, helps guide the work piece along the fence.) To finish the cut, change the fence to ⅝" to the outside of the blade and the blade height to ⅜", and push the piece through lying flat. Test cut a scrap piece, then cut the rabbets along the top edge of both end pieces.

Rip a 15° miter along the edge of a 2-ft. long 1 × 4 or 1 × 6, then cut it into 1½" × 5" handles. Measure and mark the handle location centered across the width of the ends and sides, 2" down from the tops. Hold the handle in position on each piece, drill two pilot holes for each handle, then screw the handles on with 1¼" deck screws.

Apply exterior glue down the inside edges of each side piece. Assemble the box and clamp it into position using bar clamps (a helper makes this process much easier). Check for square and adjust the box if necessary while the glue is still wet.

Drill pilot holes along the face of the side pieces, where they overlap the edges of the ends. Drive a few 2" screws near the top to hold the sides together, then remove the clamps and add the rest of the screws, spacing them about every 2".

(continued)

Rip the side and end trim pieces down to 1¼" wide. You can cut all the pieces from one 72" 1 × 2. Cut a ¼" dado at the center along one edge of each trim piece (set the fence at ¼" from the blade). Use a dado blade or just make a few passes with a regular blade. The dado should be ⁵⁄₁₆" deep.

Cut the rabbets on the ends of the end pieces using the table saw. The rabbets are cut 1¼" deep by ¾" in wide. Use a simple sliding jig made from a 2 × 6 and a clamp to complete the 1¼" cut. Then set the two boards on edge and make the ¾" cut using the sliding miter gauge. Make sure to move the fence away from the board so that the cutoff pieces don't bind and jam against the blade.

Measure and mark centerlines on the plywood cover. Mark a 4 × 1½" opening at the center of the board. Drill starter holes at the corners and cut out this hole using a jigsaw. Smooth the edges with sandpaper.

Dry fit all the pieces together and make adjustments as necessary. Lay a bead of glue in the dadoes and assemble the cover, clamping it tightly with bar clamps. When the glue has dried, drill pilot holes through the outside edge of the rabbets on the end pieces, into the ends of the side pieces. Screw them together with 1⅝" deck screws.

Drill pilot holes through the side faces into the ends of the end pieces for the butt joints. Screw the top frame together using two 1⅝" deck screws per joint. Check for square as you work to ensure the frame will exactly align with the top.

Align the top to the frame on all sides, then screw the top down with predrilled 1¼" deck screws on all sides.

Use the frame upside down to mark the bend lines on the sheet metal top, then cut out the 45° corners. Place the metal over the top and clamp it firmly in place at the bend line with a straight 2 × 4. Bend the edge over with a piece of wood, then use a rubber mallet to make the bend sharper.

Screw or nail the metal top to the wood sides with ¾" galvanized fasteners spaced every few inches.

INDEX

For even more information on improving your own home or homestead, visit **www.wholehomenews.com** today! From raising vegetables to raising roofs, it's the one-stop spot for sharing questions and getting answers about the challenges of self-sufficient living.

Brought to you by two publishing imprints of the Quayside Publishing Group, Voyageur Press and Cool Springs Press, *Whole Home News* is a blog for people interested in the same things we are: self-sufficiency, gardening, home improvement, country living, and sustainability. Our mission is to provide you with information on the latest techniques and trends from industry experts and everyday enthusiasts.

In addition to regular posts written by our volunteer in-house advisory committee, you'll also meet others from the larger enthusiast community dedicated to "doing it for ourselves." Some of these contributors include published authors of bestselling books, magazine and newspaper journalists, freelance writers, media personalities, and industry experts. And you'll also find features from ordinary folks who are equally passionate about these topics.

Join us at **www.wholehomenews.com** to keep the conversation going. You can also shoot us an email at wholehomenews@quaysidepub.com. We look forward to seeing you online, and thanks for reading!